SECOND EDITION

The Articulate Attorney

Public Speaking for Lawyers

Praise for *The Articulate Attorney* and Johnson & Hunter

"The information in Johnson & Hunter's *The Articulate Attorney* is simple to follow and its advice easily implemented. The book is well organized, logically set out, and the summaries valued without being unnecessarily repetitive. The helpful tips and advice provided by *The Articulate Attorney* have given me the confidence to step out and be a leader in my field. I find myself thinking about upcoming speaking engagements with anticipation now, rather than dread."

—Thomas Cohen, Partner, Alston + Bird, Los Angeles, CA

"Providing more than a powerful toolkit, Johnson and Hunter convey, in simple language and easily appreciated metaphors, just enough science for you to understand how to skillfully use your body's hardwiring and your brain's operating system to maximum advantage."

— Michael Halberstam, Associate Professor of Law,
SUNY Buffalo Law School, Buffalo, NY

"Practical, entertaining advice for every lawyer on how to use your body, mind, and voice to be an effective and confident speaker. Easy step-by-step exercises to help you understand and apply these techniques for skillful communication. When I noticed myself swaying during an important presentation, their mantra 'Plant your feet and stand still' came to mind and I immediately felt more relaxed and confident."

— Teri Taylor, Arizona Women Lawyers Association

"*The Articulate Attorney* will lead you to embrace opportunities for public speaking. It offers thoughtful, original, and convincing techniques for oral communication. Crucial topics that few authors would think to consider—such as what to do with your hands and feet, how to practice your presentation, and that PowerPoint can be either a visual aid or a hindrance—are explained usefully. And the book is fun to read because the authors' personalities come across. Your listeners will be able to connect better with you too, and will like you personally, if you follow the path of *The Articulate Attorney*."

— William J. Wernz, Of Counsel, Dorsey, Minneapolis, MN

SECOND EDITION

The Articulate Attorney

Public Speaking for Lawyers

Brian K. Johnson and Marsha Hunter

CROWN KING BOOKS

Copyright © 2010, 2013 by Crown King Books
Published by Crown King Books
a division of Crown King Media, L.L.C.

    Johnson, Brian K.
        The articulate attorney : public speaking for lawyers
     / Brian K. Johnson and Marsha Hunter. -- 2nd ed.
        p. cm.
        Includes bibliographical references and index.
        ISBN 978-0-9796895-9-8
        ISBN 978-1-939506-99-3
        ISBN 978-1-939506-98-6
        ISBN 978-1-939506-97-9

     1. Forensic oratory. 2. Public speaking.
    3. Communication in law--United States. 4. Lawyers--United
States--Handbooks, manuals, etc.   I. Hunter, Marsha.
    II. Title.

    K181.J64 2013   347'.075
                   QBI13-600030

Cover design by Charles Kreloff
Book design and Illustrations by Barbara Richied

Crown King Books
600 North Fourth Street
Phoenix, AZ 85004
crownkingbooks.com

There are two types of speakers:
those that are nervous and those that are liars.

Mark Twain

Contents

Foreword. 1

Introduction 5

CHAPTER ONE

Your Body 9

Understanding Adrenaline 10

The Ultimate Performance Ritual 12

Controlling Your Lower Body 14

Plant Your Feet 15

Stand Still 16

Flexible Knees 16

Center Your Hips 17

Move with a Purpose 19

Conscious, Controlled Breathing 21

The Mechanics of Conscious Breathing 22

Breathe In and Speak Out 24

Oxygenate Your Thinking Brain 25

What Do You Do with Your Hands? 25

The Science of Natural Gestures 26

The Art of Natural Gestures 28

Jump-Start Your Own Gestures. 29

Get the Feel of It First 29

The Zone of Gesture 30

The Impulse to Gesture. 32

**What Do You Do with Your Hands
When You Are Not Gesturing?** 33
The Ready Position 34
The "Invisible" Ready Position 35
Never Say Never 36
The Mechanics of Readiness 36
The Secret Handshake. 37
Don't Hold a Pen 38
Some Gestures are Distracting. 39

The Three Rs of Natural Gesture 40
Give, Chop, and Show 41
Gesture "On the Shelf". 46
Summing Up Gestures 49

Posture and Alignment. 49
Your Neck and Head. 50
Align Your Spine 50
Speaking While Sitting 52

Your Face 53
Your Mouth 53
Your Furrowed Brow 54
Eye Contact. 55
Eyes and Notes 58

Summary 59

Talk to Yourself. 60

CHAPTER TWO

Your Brain
. 61

Adrenaline and the Time Warp 62
Seeking the Zone of Concentration. 65
Echo Memory. 67

Thinking on Your Feet. 68
Do Not Read. 68
Do Not Recite. 69
Structured Improvisation. 69
Do Not Read and Talk Simultaneously 71
Notes as Your Visual Aid 71
Plan to Forget 80
Scripting as a Preliminary Step 83
Avoid Thinking Backward. 83
Chunking 84

Structure: Primacy and Recency 85

Attitude is a Tactical Choice. 88

Mirror Neurons 90

What About PowerPoint? 91

Summary 96

Talk to Yourself. 97

CHAPTER THREE

Your Voice

. 99

Listening to Yourself 100

Your Lungs and Diaphragm 101
Intercostal Muscles and Your Ribcage 102
Project Your Voice with Breath 103
Vocal Fatigue. 104
Your Larynx and Vocal Cords 105
Articulators and Articulation. 105
Warm Up to Be Articulate. 106

Making Expressive Choices 109
Energy Up, Pace Down 109
Speak in Phrases, Not Whole Sentences. 110
The Mechanics of Phrasing 112
Vary the Pace. 114
Use Your First Utterances to Set the Pace. 115
Begin Sentences Deliberately. 117

Eliminate Thinking Noises 117
Mind the Gap 119

Emphasis and Meaning 120
Volume, Pitch and Duration 124
When You Must Read 126

Gestures and Emphasis 127
Monotone. 128
Conduct Yourself. 129
Be Smooth 129
Practice Beginnings with Gestures 130
Visualize Your Performance 132

Prosody: The Music of Natural Conversation 133
Audible Punctuation 134

Practicing Verbal Skills 136

Summary 137

Talk to Yourself 138

CHAPTER FOUR

How to Practice 139

To Know vs. Know How 141

Practice: Resistance and Avoidance. 142

Practicing with a Mirror 142
Rationalizations that Inhibit Practicing 143
Be Patient 144

How to Practice Step-by-Step 144
Practice in the Actual Room 145
Run Your Body's Checklist 146
Warm Up Your Voice 147
Speak in Phrases 147
Gesture Immediately 148
Talk First and Write Second 148
Practice Your Beginning 148
Practice Your Ending 149
Practice Transitions 150
When You Must Read Aloud: Practice! 150
When You Recite from Memory 151
Notes and Visual Aids 152
Make a Video 154

Exercises to Solve Specific Problems 155

Informal Practice Sessions 160
Practice During Everyday Conversations 161
Observe, Adapt, Adopt 161
The Law of Opposites 162

Practicing for the Mental Challenge 163
One Final Thought 164

Summary 165

Talk to Yourself 167

Appendices 169

Appendix One 171
Speaker's Checklist 171

Appendix Two 175
Video Self-Review Checklist 175

Bibliography 179

Index 181

About the Authors 187

For our supportive siblings, Bruce and Jeanne.

Foreword

I n the early '90s, I had the opportunity to observe one of the greatest Texas trial lawyers, Joe Jamail, in action. It was like watching fireworks on the Fourth of July. He ignited the courtroom with his voice and gestures to advocate for the client while simultaneously burying the opposing party. And although he often used colorful antics to make a point, it was the strategic use of his body, brain, and voice— all in tandem—that persuaded the jury to vote in his favor. Shortly after that experience, I joined an AmLaw 50 law firm as the head of lawyer recruitment and development. Mistakenly, I thought all lawyers would naturally have the same commanding, persuasive communication style. Now having hired and developed thousands of lawyers in top law firms across the country for over two decades, I realize just how wrong I was. Great communicators are not just born. They are developed through practice and training.

The Most Critical Lawyering Skill

It is a mistake to think that the need for communication skills is confined to trial lawyers or litigation attorneys. Communication skills are the *foundation* for any successful lawyer in any field. In fact, research conducted by Lawyer Metrics with over 1,000 lawyers reveals that oral communication skills ranks as one of the top "most critical traits" for high-performing lawyers.

Research shows that a high intellect is only half of the equation behind legal success. Lawyers are judged not only by the content of their message, but also by how that content is delivered. A lawyer who lacks the ability to influence the listener—whether it's the client, the company board, the judge, or the opposing counsel—will not be *perceived* to be as smart or as effective as a lawyer with sharp communication capabilities. Great communication skills instill confidence in the listener—giving the speaker and the content more authority.

Instilling confidence in the listener is not just an important skill used in courtrooms or other structured settings, it's a necessary daily skill. Junior lawyers must convince partners with every conversation that they are both intelligent enough and confident enough to do their clients' most prized work. In-house lawyers have to assure their management that they are addressing the company's important legal needs. All of these interactions require confident, articulate, and persuasive oral communication. Any lawyer without this skill set is missing a valuable opportunity to advance his or her career—even if the lawyer otherwise has the necessary intellectual tools.

But how, as a new or experienced lawyer, can you gain this ability? You could wait and hone these skills through decades of trial and error—finally achieving your status as a great communicator in the twilight of your career. Or you could accelerate your learning through tried and tested techniques taught by respected experts in the field of communication.

That's where Brian, Marsha, and this book come into play.

How to Become the Articulate Attorney

Whether you have to address a massive audience about healthcare law or merely give a quick overview of the deal you're working on to a group of partners, I strongly encourage you to read, internalize, and emulate *The Articulate Attorney*. Brian and Marsha have distilled their techniques into a set of simple instructions that any lawyer can use to enhance his or her presentation style and communication skills.

The book starts with the effective use of one's body when communicating. This is the nonverbal part of communication we often neglect. Watch a video of yourself presenting without the sound and you will understand what I mean. How you stand, when you move, where you place your hands—all of these actions have an effect on whether or not you are perceived as confident and persuasive. And, interestingly, studies have shown that "how you look" when communicating has a bigger impact on first impressions than what you say or how you say it.

Chapters Two and Three tackle the significant roles that your brain and voice play in the process. Very few people have the ability to "speak well while they think on their feet" when they have to organize complex information in their head and deliver it simultaneously. That is why we have all experienced the agony of speakers who read their speeches verbatim or rely so heavily on their notes that they never look up. Brian and Marsha provide techniques to help lawyers use their notes and visuals more effectively while commanding the attention of the room through the varied use of volume, tone, and pace. They also teach lawyers to talk in short phrases. After all, you don't have the luxury of commas, colons, and other punctuation when you speak. You have to create space and moments of rest for your listener's mind to truly digest what you are saying.

The final chapter suggests methods for applying these body, brain, and voice lessons in unison through practice. As explained in mounds of empirical research and books, such as Malcolm Gladwell's book *The Outliers*, deliberate practice is the best method for becoming an expert at almost anything. This is a skill you use daily; why not consciously practice good techniques daily?

Deliberate Practice Makes Perfect

Over the last two decades, I have had the pleasure of hiring Brian and Marsha to teach these skills at many firms and found their communication techniques, teaching style, and unique expertise to be highly valuable and effective for all lawyers, no matter their experience level, practice group, or geographic region. Anytime Brian and Marsha were on my firms' training calendars, I could expect to have a long wait list of eager participants, especially partners. The most successful partners knew from experience—both good and bad—that enhancing their oral communication skills was the one of the most useful and beneficial steps they could take to win business, persuade a board, or convince a judge to grant a motion.

Brian and Marsha have taken the skills they teach so effectively in person and created a step-by-step guide to using your body and your voice—in combination with your brain—to command the attention of an audience, no matter how large or small.

This book should definitely be one of the most read, re-read, and earmarked books on a lawyer's bookshelf.

Caren Ulrich Stacy
President & Principal, Lawyer Metrics LLC
Adjunct Faculty, University of Denver Sturm College of Law

Introduction

People expect attorneys to be good public speakers. How do we know this? When we tell people we teach public speaking to attorneys, the inevitable response is a slight chuckle of surprise, followed by: "Do they really need that?"

Outside the legal profession people tend to think that all lawyers are good speakers because they believe, mistakenly, that all attorneys are trial lawyers who regularly appear in court. Others presume that all attorneys speak as fluidly as the articulate, confident actors who portray trial lawyers on film and television—which, after all, forms the public's most common frame of reference for the profession, albeit an inaccurate one. In fact, many non-lawyers believe you can't even get into law school unless you pass a test proving that you are a verbally aggressive personality, and, therefore, a gifted speaker.

But you know better. We've talked with thousands of attorneys over the years and it's become apparent that some law students decide to become corporate and transactional lawyers precisely because they have *no* desire to stand up and speak—ever—and especially not in a courtroom!

Sooner or later, almost all attorneys realize that speaking in public is part of the job. Maybe you have to stand in your firm's conference room and speak to your colleagues; or use your expertise to teach a CLE program in a hotel ballroom; or market your firm to potential clients. Perhaps you find yourself standing in your client's boardroom, speaking to the board of directors; or addressing the local zoning council on behalf of a client; or making a fundraising appeal for the non-profit organization that asked you to be on their board—because, of course, all lawyers can speak well, which is one reason they asked you to serve.

If this hasn't happened yet, your time is coming. Here's the good news: if you are smart enough to get through law school, pass the bar, and become a lawyer, you are smart enough to become an articulate attorney capable of speaking to any group, in any setting, on any topic that you know well. All it takes is the desire to learn the technique that makes it possible. Even if you are one of those lawyers who never, ever wanted to be a public speaker, you can become a proficient and polished presenter. This book will provide you with the necessary technique; you supply the determination to put it into practice.

The Paradox of Naturalness

Good public speaking is not based on pretending, acting, or faking it; you must look, sound, and feel authentic to appear confident, comfortable and credible. It may seem logical simply to tell yourself to "be natural" or "be yourself," but that is only part of the solution—for the challenge of being natural is complicated by a surprising paradox.

The word "natural" has many definitions: here it refers to the way you speak, think, and behave regularly and consistently in the course of daily life. If you do something often, it's natural; if you don't, it's not. Some of these natural behaviors will make you look and feel *unnatural* while giving presentations to a group. And as a speaker you need to consciously employ certain *unnatural* behaviors in order to look and feel natural. Thus, the paradox!

To complicate the issue, most people remain unaware of their natural behaviors due to this polarity in human behavior: When you are natural, you are not self-conscious. When you are self-conscious, you don't feel natural. Therefore, you can't just tell yourself to "be natural" while speaking, because it is unlikely you are fully conscious of what your natural behavior is. What you need is technique.

Your Body

Consider some of the physical behaviors you display while engaged in everyday conversation. As you speak with a colleague, you unconsciously exhibit certain mannerisms. Perhaps you push your eyeglasses up on your nose, or brush your hair from your face. You may jingle the change in your pocket, fiddle with a pen, or shift your weight back and forth from one leg to the other. Neither you nor your colleague is likely to be aware of, or distracted by, these behaviors. They are normal, unconscious, and natural.

Now imagine that you are standing up to speak in public. You tell yourself to be natural, and your body follows that instruction exactly. The audience watches you shift your weight back and forth, push your glasses up on your nose, brush your hair from your brow, fiddle with your pen, and jingle the change in your pocket. Do these behaviors make you look "natural" to your listeners? No, far from it.

Under the intense scrutiny of public speaking, the paradox of naturalness emerges and causes your perfectly normal behaviors to look unnatural. When energizing adrenaline is added to the experience, your body unconsciously engages in these natural actions with extra vigor. More frequent rocking, shifting, pushing, brushing, fidgeting, and jingling make you look increasingly uncomfortable and unnatural. Natural mannerisms that go unnoticed elsewhere appear conspicuous and unnatural. What a paradox! Clearly, "being natural" is not the best method for discovering your personal style.

Your Brain

Another example of this paradox relates to your thought process. In conversation you engage in a natural exchange of ideas, back and forth, between two people. However, you may be asked to address an audience for, perhaps, an hour. That's unnatural! When do you ever have a conversation in which you speak for an hour nonstop before saying to your friend or colleague, "What do *you* think?" (Never, one hopes!)

As a result, it is not natural for your brain to structure, remember, and speak nonstop about something for an hour. That's the cognitive challenge a public speaker faces.

Your Voice

You must be able to speak loudly enough for your voice to fill the room and be audible to all listeners. If you are a soft-spoken person by nature, this may feel completely unnatural to you. Yet, should someone in the back row bark, "Please speak up—we can't hear you," you can't respond, "Sorry, that wouldn't be natural for me." Authoritative audibility is required, whether it is natural for you or not.

Further, you must be able to control the pace at which you speak; rid your speech of "thinking noises;" assess how well your audience understands even your most complex ideas; and choose the right word when the pressure is on. The ability to make conscious decisions about using your voice and speaking with finesse is a requirement for public speaking.

Technique

Clearly, just "being yourself" won't make you a good speaker, nor will instructing yourself to "be natural." To discover your authentic, personal style, you need a solid technique that will provide you with reliable answers to all those challenging questions about how to look, sound, and feel natural in front of an audience. How you control your body influences your ability to use your brain to remember and your voice to speak clearly. As you develop and refine this technique, you pass through self-consciousness to self-awareness, and finally, to self-control. Once you have mastered a technique, the skills of public speaking become second nature.

CHAPTER ONE

Your Body

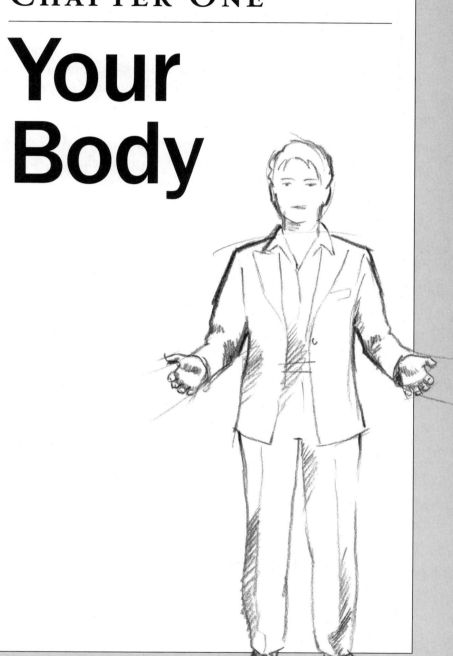

I n public speaking, the goal is to look confident, comfortable, and credible when you stand up to address an audience. The way you stand, move, breathe, gesture, and focus your gaze significantly affects how listeners perceive you. Audiences unconsciously scrutinize your physical behavior as they listen, and if your demeanor signals nervousness and discomfort, it will make them feel ill at ease too. But if you act confident and enthusiastic, listeners will concentrate on your topic, not you. To achieve this initial goal—looking dynamically at ease and believable at all times, even when feeling nervous—requires a fail-safe technique for controlling your body.

Understanding the function of adrenaline is likewise of paramount importance to your development as a speaker; few things have greater impact on your performance. Feelings of anxiety and excitement inevitably trigger the flow of adrenaline, which sends excess energy coursing through your system. This leads many speakers to pace or sway, breathe fast and shallow, gesture awkwardly, and fidget with their hands. Even the eyes are affected by adrenaline: nervous energy makes it hard for them to focus, and they tend to flit around the room, depriving the audience of eye contact and the speaker of concentration. However, by learning to control your breath as well as the movement of your legs, arms, hands, and eyes, you can channel the power of adrenaline and dictate how your body responds to it.

With guided practice, you will discover how to instruct your body to act in an appropriate and effective way. You can gain conscious control of your body by making desired behaviors part of a performance ritual. You will then look comfortable and confident from the very beginning of every presentation, regardless of how you may feel.

Understanding Adrenaline

Adrenaline is a natural hormone released by the adrenal glands. It flows through the body when your instinct signals a need for extra energy, perhaps to defend yourself, run away, or respond to the pressure of performance. Performance pressures often take a positive form, such as excitement or anticipation. When athletes talk of "being pumped" for the big game, they are responding to that adrenaline being pumped, literally, by their bodies in anticipation of performance. Adrenaline also assists athletes by producing the extra energy needed to throw a ball farther or run faster, and by helping them to concentrate and focus the mind in the heat of competition. Likewise, adrenaline can be a positive factor while speaking.

The body also pumps adrenaline in response to negative pressures, such as nervousness, anxiety, and panic. Excess nervous energy is often referred to as the fight-or-flight syndrome, because adrenaline energizes and animates muscles in our arms to help us fight and in our legs to help us flee.

Although our need to outrun predators has been reduced in modern society, thankfully, we're all familiar with adrenaline-induced energy: it makes your limbs tremble. If you stand up to speak and feel your hands shaking, this is the result of adrenaline preparing your arm muscles to fight. If you feel your knees knocking, adrenaline is pumping extra energy into your thighs and quadriceps to prepare you to run from a threat. The trembling occurs because every muscle in the body is paired with another muscle—for example, biceps and triceps work together to move your forearm—and when adrenaline energizes both simultaneously, they tense and pull against each other, causing the arms or legs to shake.

The common form of nervousness known as "having butterflies in your stomach" takes place in muscles of respiration. The flutter of those metaphorical butterflies occurs when the diaphragm and intercostal muscles in the ribs pull against each other in response to adrenaline. As you speak, you feel a flutter, which sometimes becomes audible. Your voice shakes or cracks when this excessive muscular tension robs you of adequate breath support, without which you will not be loud enough to be heard. Chances are good you will be so distracted by these butterflies that you won't be your most articulate self.

For many speakers, adrenaline pumps because of an ever-shifting balance between excitement and nervousness. It is not only invigorating to confront the challenge of speaking effectively, it is nerve-wracking—

often just a little, sometimes quite a lot. Even experienced speakers admit they experience this phenomenon. Although it is impossible to predict how much adrenaline you will generate at any given moment, it is guaranteed that you will feel the effect of at least some. Regardless of its source, the secret is to channel adrenaline's corresponding energy in the most effective and appropriate way.

If adrenaline isn't channeled and released, it triggers various inappropriate, unconscious mannerisms that make you look and feel ill at ease. However, if you learn to recognize the impulses to fight, flee, or freeze, you can counter adrenaline's negative effects by proactively gaining control of specific parts of your body.

Conscious control of your behavior can be established by counting several seconds of silence after you stand up but before you begin to speak. You may feel an extra rush of adrenaline as you face your listeners. During the silence, run through a short physical checklist designed to help you prepare your body and focus your mind. Olympic athletes use just such an anticipatory silence as they prepare to dive into a pool, ski down a mountain, or race around a track. Like the preparatory rituals used by these elite athletes, you will develop your own practice.

The Ultimate Performance Ritual

In 1992, a 72-year-old retiree walked onto a basketball court in Riverside, California, and made 2,750 consecutive free throws without a miss. Dr. Tom Amberry—who had such confidence in his technique that he brought along 10 witnesses to sign affidavits for his submission to the Guinness Book of World Records—readily admits he is not a great athlete, and never was. So how did he accomplish such a feat? He had great technique.

In his book *Free Throw: 7 Steps to Success at the Free Throw Line*, Amberry describes the mental and physical ritual that gave him such astonishing control and consistency. Every move Dr. Amberry made prior to each throw was part of an unvarying routine. During the silence between throws, he went through a physical checklist. How he planted his feet, how he breathed, how many times he bounced the ball, how his fingers held the ball, how he focused his eyes on the basket—every move was precisely the same all 2,750 times. Because this ritual was so consistent, he achieved remarkable results on the basketball court. As demonstrated by Amberry's amazing feat, consistent ritual and other discoveries of sports psychology can help you achieve success in public speaking.

Sports psychologists teach that if you want to perform at a high level, you need a consistent mental and physical ritual on which to base your performance. This is to enable the mind, through repetition and practice, to control the body, and to enable the body to control the mind. Together, body and mind help control emotion.

To achieve a consistently effective style, devise and refine a physical ritual that you can use every time you stand up to speak. In time, this routine will become "second nature"—behavior that looks natural, but is actually the result of technique and diligent practice.

Reliance on a physical ritual frees your brain's prefrontal cortex (the area of your brain responsible for higher intellectual function) from being distracted by pacing, fidgeting, or gesturing, and ensures that your body's actions will be governed by your motor cortex, the brain's overseer of natural automatic functions. Your prefrontal cortex can focus then on more important things, such as what you want to say and how you want to say it. Hence, by ritualizing your physical actions, you have engaged your instinct to move and gesture naturally.

For your own ritual, start with your feet and move up the body to your head. Use a mental checklist to position and align your body: feet, knees, hips, breath, arms, face, and eyes. Running through this quick checklist will help you get control of your body, positioning and aligning it for optimum performance every time you stand to speak.

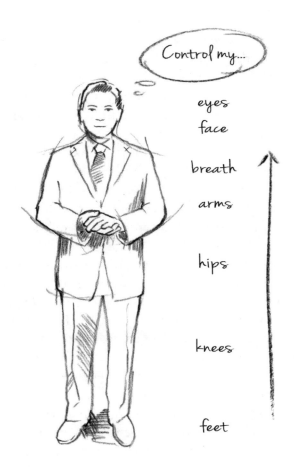

Think from the bottom up, focusing briefly on each part of your body. As you do this, become conscious of the details of your alignment. Use your own body as a mnemonic device to memorize your physical ritual.

Controlling Your Lower Body

In most sports, athletes start by planting their feet in the proper stance. The golfer adopts a stance and then swings a club. The baseball player ritualistically plants both feet in the batter's box and then swings a bat.

The basketball player positions himself on the free throw line and then shoots the ball. Similarly, public speakers begin by planting their feet on the floor.

Plant Your Feet

Stand with your feet a comfortable distance apart. Don't place them so close together that your shoes touch; this stance is too narrow for a solid, comfortable foundation. Do not adopt a stance that is too wide or you will look like a gunslinger in a Western; somewhere between the extremes of too narrow and too wide is a stance that is just right. Avoid standing with your feet in perfect parallel position, as if you are gliding along on skis. Such perfect symmetry can make you look slightly square and wooden, like a soldier at attention. Don't cross your ankles, which looks too casual. Instead, try planting one foot—whichever one feels more comfortable—an inch or two ahead of the other, with your feet slightly asymmetrical and out of alignment with each other. Slight asymmetry of the stance makes the body look more relaxed.

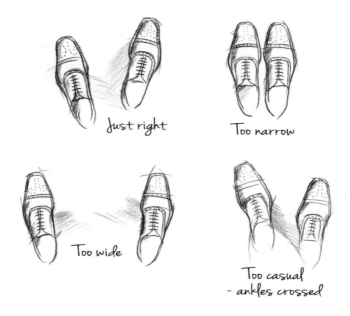

Just right

Too narrow

Too wide

Too casual
- ankles crossed

Stand up and experiment right now with finding the right stance. Better yet, stand in front of a floor-length mirror so you can see how your stance looks. Once you are satisfied, use it every time you stand up to speak. Soon it will become second nature, and your body, just like an athlete's, will assume the position automatically, without your needing to think about it.

Plant your feet in the moment before you speak. Do not utter a word until you have planted your feet and are standing still. Then, pause for another moment, take a breath, and feel the floor.

Stand Still

Newton's first law of motion applies to public speaking: *A body at rest tends to remain at rest; a body in motion tends to remain in motion.* When you plant your feet and stand still, you look calm, comfortable, and in control, and your body will tend to stay at rest. If you start talking while your feet are still moving, your body tends to stay in motion, and may never stop. Random movement will make you appear nervous and ill at ease. Because adrenaline energizes your leg muscles, it is natural—but undesirable—to rock unconsciously, sway, pace, or shuffle your feet. So obey Newton's Law by planting your feet and standing still at the beginning of a presentation.

Flexible Knees

The next step in the ritual is to align and balance your knees and hips over your feet. Your knees should feel flexible. Don't lock your knees by pushing them backward, tightening the thigh muscles and drawing your kneecaps upward. The desirable sensation of flexibility is a feeling of the knee joint floating perfectly balanced. Think of it as "subway knees," similar to the adjustment you make when standing on public transportation as the door closes and the bus or subway is about to move. You flex your knees ever so slightly to maintain your balance when you feel forward movement. The adjustment is subtle and virtually invisible. The knees do not bend as in a crouch, but adjust enough to flexibly absorb the forward lurch of the train as it pulls out of the station.

With flexible knees your legs will feel comfortable, even when standing still for long periods of time. Stand up and briefly experiment to find this subtle feeling. Lock your knees backward and feel the sensation you want to avoid. Crouch slightly to move the knees in the opposite direction. Now find the perfect midpoint where the knee joint is floating and flexible. On the checklist, add these flexible knees to your planted feet as you continue to move up your body.

Center Your Hips

Center your hips over your feet and knees. This balances the weight of your torso evenly over both legs, allowing each leg to share the load equally. Although it may feel comfortable to stand with your body weight and hips shifted temporarily off to one side, this off-center position puts most of your body's weight onto a single leg. Eventually that leg gets tired and your body shifts the weight to your other leg. Soon your body is rocking side to side, as each leg in turn tires and shifts the burden to the other. This rocking motion distracts the audience and makes you look nervous. Note that some looseness and flexibility of the body is desirable, however; you shouldn't feel as if you've been sunk in concrete. So, avoid both repetitive rocking and absolute rigidity.

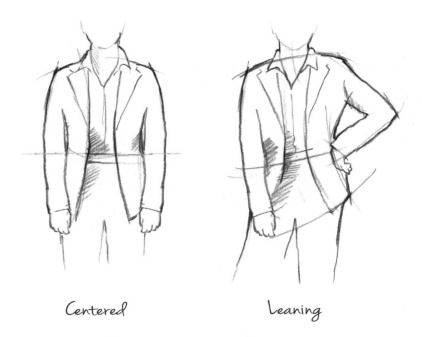

Centered   Leaning

For women wearing high heels, be aware that they can subtly shift your weight forward onto your toes, causing the buttocks to shift backwards and up. This position shortens and tenses the muscles of your lower back. To counteract this, consciously center the pelvis over your feet and rotate it forward slightly—dancers refer to this as "tucking the tail bone." This will lengthen and relax the muscles in your lower back.

Once you have planted your feet, softened your knees, and centered your hips, you have conscious control of the biggest muscles of your body: buttocks, thighs, and calves. This allows you to control your adrenaline and stand still, even if you are feeling nervous. When you first stand up, start by standing still, and then later on make a conscious decision about when and where to move, assuming that choice makes sense. If you have the freedom to move, and it makes sense to do so, move with a purpose.

Move with a Purpose

Any movement made while speaking should be motivated by and connected to your words and ideas. A purposeful move occurs when you walk to a new location while beginning to discuss a new topic: "We've explored the changes in the regulations, now let's talk about the effect of those changes on your clients." Or, "I've talked about patents, now I want to focus on licensing agreements." Once you have reached the new location, remain there until you have finished discussing the new topic. Such a purposeful use of movement clarifies the structure of your presentation for the audience. The move signals a new beginning, and helps to recapture the attention of any listeners whose minds might have wandered. It invites a distracted listener to re-engage.

Your decision to move must always be made by the thinking brain, not the adrenalized leg muscles. The largest muscles in your body will move of their own accord when they are energized by adrenaline. Powered by instinct and hormones, such movement is truly natural—but it doesn't make you look natural, and it certainly isn't desirable. Random movement may feel good because it uses and dissipates the adrenaline in your legs. But resist random movement; move only when it makes sense.

Movement has power if it starts from stillness, because the change from stasis to motion attracts attention. Incessant pacing robs movement of its impact. Don't be fooled into believing that constant motion keeps listeners interested. And don't be misled by the frequent moves of speakers on television. When television performers move around, the camera follows the action, giving the shot visual variety. The camera does the work, not the viewer: the television stays in place and the viewers' eyes barely move at all. In everyday life, when listeners are forced to watch a pacing speaker, they must do the work of the camera, panning back and forth as if tracking a ball in a tennis match. They quickly tire of following a moving target.

Aimless pacing creates visual monotony. The constant back and forth, rhythmic as a hypnotist's watch, can put listeners to sleep. When you pace, you spend half the time with your back to half of the listeners, depending on the size and position of your audience. Every time you turn around and pace in the opposite direction, you turn your back on the others. They will get bored looking at your backside, rather than your face! Hard-of-hearing or deaf listeners reading your lips will be excluded.

It is better to plant your feet and stand still in a central location facing the audience. When you make a purposeful move to a new location, and are standing still once again, listeners can see your face and you can look them in the eye. Sustained eye contact—a key element of style—is impossible if you pace back and forth.

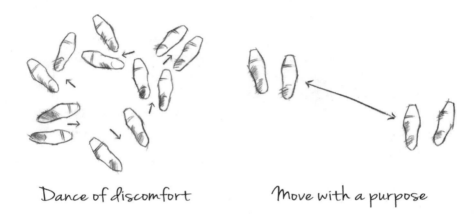

Dance of discomfort   Move with a purpose

How much movement you use, however, is very much a matter of personal style. There are excellent presenters who rarely move, while other equally effective communicators do so frequently. Make logical decisions about when and where you will move. Choose the topic areas—usually the most important ones—where you plan to move, in order to signal a transition into that discussion. You can plan these moves in advance and practice to make sure they work for you, or you can follow your instinct, live in the moment, and decide on the spot whether moving is the proper choice. Movement is a stylistic choice; it is neither a necessity nor a requirement for effective public speaking. If movement doesn't feel right to you, don't bother.

Once you have mastered the ability to plant your feet, float the knees, center the hips, stand still, and move with a purpose, you have conscious control of your body from your waist down to your feet. You are in control of your position in the room. The next step is to focus on the middle of your body—the lower torso—where deep breathing occurs.

Conscious, Controlled Breathing

One of the most useful techniques to ritualize is also the simplest: to breathe consciously. The way you breathe is directly related to the way you feel, speak, and think. Once you learn to mindfully control your breathing, it will help you calm down, project your voice, and oxygenate your brain. These three significant benefits flow from controlling how you breathe.

The technique of using breath to control emotions is widely understood. When someone is upset we often say, "You're upset—take a deep breath." Indeed, a few deep breaths have a calming effect because breath and emotion are directly connected. When we are relaxed and at ease, we breathe with longer inhalations and slower exhalations. When we are nervous, anxious, or panic-stricken, adrenaline accelerates our rate of breathing.

Right now, as you read this book, you are breathing unconsciously. If you accelerate the speed of your breathing while reading this sentence, you will begin to feel this connection between breath and emotion. Do it: breathe faster and shallower. The faster you breathe, the more it triggers an emotional response. Now breathe even faster and louder as you continue to read, and begin to simulate the respiratory action of panic. The action begins to provoke the feeling. If you breathe as if you are nervous (fast and shallow), you begin to feel nervous. No wonder—you're hyperventilating!

Fortunately, the reverse is also true. If you breathe as if you are comfortable and at ease (even when you're not), you can help to control your nervousness. If you take long, deep breaths, as you would while lying on a lawn chair during a vacation, you can provoke the feeling of greater comfort. You breathe like you feel, and you feel like you breathe. If you breathe using longer inhalations and exhalations, you imitate the action of your body's respiratory system when you are most comfortable. Take a few full, relaxing, conscious breaths as you continue reading. Feel the difference. The action of low, deliberate breathing provokes the feeling of greater comfort. While this technique does not make nervousness vanish, it can help take the edge off the anxiety you may feel before you stand to speak.

When you are breathing naturally, your respiratory system is controlled by your autonomic nervous system. This is the same system that regulates your beating heart, blinking eyes, and other vital functions. But you can override the autonomic nervous system at any moment, and take control of your respiratory system. When you do so, conscious breathing calms you down and you will feel better.

The Mechanics of Conscious Breathing

Your lungs are located in your upper torso, protected by your ribcage. Your diaphragm, which does most of the work of breathing, is a dome-shaped muscle underneath the lungs and atop the vital organs in the lower torso. When you draw a breath into your lungs, your diaphragm muscle flattens downward toward your waist, creating a partial vacuum that pulls air into your lungs. When the diaphragm moves down, the abdominal wall moves forward and the intercostal muscles pull the ribcage outward slightly. As your lungs fill with air your internal organs are pushed down and forward as the diaphragm flattens. This is why a full breath comes from the lower torso, even though your lungs are in your upper torso. It is your abdominal wall or belly that moves forward during this type of breathing. When you take a deep breath, you should feel your stomach push forward gently against the belt or waistband of your clothing. This is not a large movement; don't be surprised at how subtle it is. Note also that the shoulders do not rise as the lungs expand. Only heavy exertion causes the upper torso and shoulders to heave up and down.

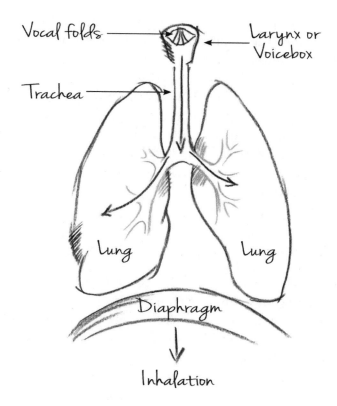

Vocal folds — Larynx or Voicebox

Trachea

Lung   Lung

Diaphragm

Inhalation

To feel the full power of this deep breathing, try this exercise: Draw a breath down into your lungs. Now empty your lungs and try to blow out every molecule of air as you exhale. Make an effort to completely empty your lungs. Keep blowing out until you feel an almost desperate need to inhale again, and then blow out the last little bit of air. Finally, when your lungs feel completely empty, breathe in. Feel the air rush back into your lungs. That is a truly deep, maximum breath. Try it again: empty your lungs as you exhale and then feel the air rush back in as you inhale. Activate the muscles of respiration that need to work long and hard when you speak to an audience. While you won't empty your lungs like this while speaking in public, it is important to understand that they have a surprising amount of untapped capacity you can use.

The sooner you gain control of your breath, the better you feel. Do not wait until you stand before an audience to think about your breathing. Get control far in advance of that moment. A few minutes before you stand up, take several deep breaths. Better still, take those mindful breaths hours earlier. As you walk to the office that day, take a few deep breaths. As you drive to the place where you are giving the speech, periodically inhale and exhale slowly, three times. When the alarm goes off in the morning and you feel that first rush of adrenaline as you think of the day's presentation, take a few deep, deliberate breaths before you get out of bed.

Breathe In and Speak Out

Once you use deliberate breathing to feel better, use that same technique to achieve your second goal: projecting your voice with authority. Chapter Three will describe more completely the connection between breathing and speaking, but it is important to mention the subject here as part of the physical ritual of preparation.

Stage actors and singers refer to the connection between breathing and speaking on the stage as "breath support." The amount of air in your lungs is what supports and projects your voice. Your voice is loud in direct proportion to the volume of air in your lungs. Less air means less sound; more air creates more sound. If you control of your breath while still sitting down, you then have more air available when you stand up to speak. If you are naturally soft spoken, there is only one way to turn up the volume: use more air. Since you need more air flowing out of your lungs to speak louder, you obviously must bring extra air into your lungs as you inhale. That air is then available to put more power behind your voice. You speak on the exhalation of breath from the lungs.

Patsy Rodenburg, the preeminent voice coach at London's Royal National Theatre, describes the mechanics of speaking as "breathe in, speak out." Breathe in to fill your lungs, then speak as the air flows back out. The breath flows up through your trachea and then the voice box, where your vocal cords are made to vibrate by the passing air. Start speaking when your lungs are full of air. Don't make the mistake of trying to speak after you have exhaled. Breathe in, and speak out once you have filled your lungs with air.

Oxygenate Your Thinking Brain

You will discover a third benefit of conscious breathing. The more efficiently you breathe, the more you increase the amount of oxygen in your lungs, which passes into your bloodstream and circulates throughout your body, including to your brain. Your brain needs about 20% of the oxygen your body takes in. The more efficiently and deeply you breathe, the more ample the supply of oxygen to your lungs, your bloodstream, and ultimately, your brain. This will help you to think quickly and clearly.

Since breathing will help you feel, speak, and think better, the sooner you begin the process of deliberate breathing and the more consistently you do it, the more control you will have. Just as planting your feet and standing still controls the adrenaline in your legs, controlling the breath prevents adrenaline from accelerating your respiration.

The next challenge is to channel and release adrenaline's considerable energy, directing it to flow appropriately out of the body. For that, you need to use your arms, hands, and shoulders.

What Do You Do with Your Hands?

Many speakers struggle with this question. Since you want to look and feel natural as you make your presentation, it may seem logical to tell yourself to simply gesture the way you always do. But that answer is not helpful, because of the paradox of naturalness discussed in the Introduction. You don't know how your own gestures function or what they look like. "Gesture naturally" is at best a partial answer.

A common yet mistaken answer to this question is, "Don't gesture." Some people cling to an old-fashioned, post-Victorian belief that gestures are inappropriate for public speaking. Law students and attorneys are often told to place their hands on the lectern or at their sides, because gestures distract the listener. There are three problems with this belief: there is no scientific evidence to back it up; it is completely unnatural to inhibit your gestures; and it is not the way effective lawyers behave while speaking. If your goal is to be natural, then standing with your arms dangling at your sides or clutching the lectern could not be a worse answer.

The assertion that gestures are distracting is an excellent example of unreliable hearsay, to use a courtroom expression. Neuroscientists and social scientists have discovered that gesture and language are inextricably intertwined in the human brain. Research in the areas of neurology and cognition proves beyond a reasonable doubt that gesturing is an integral component of speaking and thinking. You must gesture in order to speak and think naturally. Gestures not only enhance the meaning of language, they allow the body to channel and release the energy of adrenaline.

Everyone gestures. Some people do it more and others less, but everyone gestures in conversation, especially when speaking with energy and enthusiasm, which is essential for public speaking. Reading this, you may be saying to yourself, "But I don't gesture! I know I don't." You may not be aware of it—yet—because your gestures are not controlled by the conscious intellect. They are controlled by instinct.

The Science of Natural Gestures

After a trip to Italy, psychologist Dr. Jana Iverson was inspired to study the origin of gesturing. Her research posed the following questions: Do we learn to gesture by watching others do it? In other words, are gestures nurtured by observation and imitation when children are learning to speak? Or is it hard-wired in the human brain—is it nature rather than nurture that makes us gesture? Iverson's research studied children who were blind from birth, observing them in conversation with others.

Dr. Iverson discovered something surprising. Congenitally blind children use gestures when they talk, even when speaking to other blind people. The blind children gestured the same as her sighted control group. How can someone gesture who has never seen a gesture? Dr. Iverson's study reveals the innate connection in the brain between the flow of gestures and the flow of language. Dr. Iverson writes, "The fact that someone who had never seen gestures before would gesture, even to a partner who they know can't see, suggests that gesturing and speaking are tightly connected in some very fundamental way in our brains." Gestures not only help speakers speak, the flow of gestures also assists listeners in understanding what is being said.

The journal *Research on Language and Social Interaction* published a special issue called *Gesture and Understanding in Social Interaction*, in which studies revealed the important connection between thinking, speaking, gesturing, and listening. One study reported that people comprehended spoken sentences *twice as well* when gestures accompanied speech as when they were absent. In another study, the subjects were told a short story and then given a partial transcript of the story and asked to fill in the missing parts. The researchers concluded: "…those parts of the story accompanied by well-defined gestures were filled in with greater accuracy." In other words, gestures will help your listeners remember what you said.

By giving subtle clues about intent and point of view—crucial components in comprehension—gestures also allow listeners to understand a speaker more thoroughly. If you want your audience to follow, remember, and be informed by your presentation, you must gesture.

Furthermore, gestures will help you remember and verbalize your intended message better. Research by Adam Kendon of the University of Pennsylvania asserts that gestures help speakers conjure the proper words from memory. The journal *Psychological Science* has reported a finding by Dr. Susan Goldin-Meadow of the University of Chicago that people who were allowed to gesture while recalling a list of memorized words recalled on average 20% more than people who were not allowed to gesture. In other words, gesturing assists word retrieval and memory. If gesturing will improve your ability to recall and remember what you want to say by a full 20%, it is obvious that gesturing is an essential element of your personal style.

Further scientific evidence of the close linkage between speech, gesture, and comprehension can be found in David McNeill's *Hand and Mind* as well as Dr. Susan Goldin-Meadow's *Hearing Gesture: How Our Hands Help Us Think*. Neurologist Frank R. Wilson's *The Hand: How Its Use Shapes the Brain, Language, and Human Culture* provides an anthropological perspective on the issue. (See our bibliography for references.)

The Art of Natural Gestures

This science of gesture dovetails precisely with the art of gesturing, as described by the greatest playwright in the English language. William Shakespeare, speaking through the title character in *Hamlet,* offers the following practical suggestion. In the speech referred to as Hamlet's Advice to the Players, Shakespeare's instructions are simple: "Suit the action to the word, the word to the action."

His advice confirms Dr. Goldin-Meadow's observation "…that gesturing and speaking are tightly connected in some very fundamental way in our brains." Art and science agree that gestures suit, or fit, the words being spoken, and the words logically fit the actions of our hands. Gesturing is not emotional or theatrical, but logical.

Put Shakespeare's logic into action with a two-step process. First, carefully choose and diligently practice the words you will say to begin your presentation. (Do not improvise your first sentences. Winging it does not work!) Second, practice fitting gestures to those words. Experiment with different options, and then select the most suitable. This will trigger the instinct that connects words to gestures and gestures to words. Do this, and you will look, sound, and feel much more natural right from the start.

Jump-Start Your Own Gestures

You have a lifetime of experience gesturing while speaking. Instinctively and unconsciously, your body already knows how to do it, but you need a technique to jump-start it from the beginning of every presentation. The challenge is to immediately liberate your hands so they can move freely, and to avoid over-intellectualizing what they do every minute. Think about your gestures to get them started; stop thinking about them once they get going.

Triggering your natural gestures is analogous to jump-starting a dead car battery. You connect jumper cables from a working battery to the dead one. The working battery jump-starts the moribund one when you turn the key in the ignition. Once the engine is running, you remove the jumper cables, slam the hood, and drive off, confident that electricity is now flowing.

At the very beginning of a presentation, the instinct to gesture can be as dead as a car battery at twenty below zero, frozen by self-consciousness, anxiety, or the erroneous belief that gestures are distracting. To jump-start your gestures, think of your brain as the energy source. Connect the metaphorical jumper cables of conscious thought to your instinct to gesture and turn the key. Deliberately gesture at the beginning, and suit the action to the word. Make sure your gestural engine is running.

Get the Feel of It First

When learning how to finger the strings of a guitar, dance the tango, or swing a golf club, you may look and feel a little awkward at first, until you get the feel of it. To learn a new physical skill, you begin by thinking intensely about the action required, a process that takes place in the prefrontal cortex of your brain. When learning to play the guitar you painstakingly think about each chord: put the index finger here, middle finger there, ring finger there, and the pinkie finger over here. You concentrate on each chord and make mistakes. Your playing feels awkward. But once you begin to get the feel of it, your motor cortex takes over. Muscle memory places your fingers on the guitar strings. You think: C major chord, and your fingers know where to go.

This conscious gesturing may not feel natural the first time you try it. Don't be surprised. The gestures are natural, but the conscious activity of the brain telling the hands to do them is unnatural. It is technical, and first you need to learn and practice the mechanics. With enough practice it becomes second nature. Unlike learning a new skill such as golf or tennis, you are triggering a primal instinct. Don't let a little initial awkwardness frustrate you. Practice the skill until you get the feel of it.

Even though you gesture in a unique personal style, some general observations apply to everybody. As you observe your gestures and those of other speakers, pay specific attention to how large they are, how long they last, and how they are connected to words. Note the specific shape of the hands while gesturing, and where hands go when they are still. Rather than focus on the faces of speakers, watch their hands.

The Zone of Gesture

Natural gestures have observable and quantifiable characteristics. For example, conversational gestures are surprisingly large. They move or flow through an area in front of the body called the "zone of gesture." This zone is a large space approximately two feet tall by four feet wide. It extends vertically from the waist to the nose. Gestures rarely happen with the hands below the waist or above the shoulders. This zone extends horizontally about two feet out to each side of your body—almost the full reach of your arms. Even when you are sitting down, your gestures regularly fill this zone.

When sitting in a mall, restaurant, or airport, watch the animated conversations taking place around you and note the size of the gestures you see. When sitting in a meeting and listening to others speak, focus on hands. Watch how people gesture on television and in films. Watch television with the sound turned off to observe gestures. You will be surprised at how large natural gestures really are. As the title of Dr. Susan Goldin-Meadow's book suggests: start *hearing* gestures. Listen to the words people are saying, but watch their hands. Observe the size of the zone of gesture, and see the obvious connection between speech and gesture.

Gestures often involve the whole arm from the shoulder to the hand. This isn't to suggest that all are large and expansive; many are not. But many use the entire limb. Extend your arms so they comfortably fill the zone.

By using your whole arm, you avoid a common pitfall of nervous speakers: gesturing with just wrists or forearms. Anxious speakers keep the upper arms tight against the body, as if the elbow has been bolted to the ribcage. This not only shrinks the zone of gesture, it limits the size of gestures, making them appear and feel unnatural. Smaller gestures are tight and jerky; the zone is shrunken and cramped. The body's instinct for self-preservation keeps the hands and forearms in front of vital organs for protection, making gestures tentative and constricted. Such half-gestures reveal a speaker's anxiety, doing nothing to clarify the meaning of speech. They don't last long enough to support and reinforce expressive speaking. The action is not suited to the word, as Shakespeare suggests.

In addition to being large and filling the zone, gestures often last a long time. Watch how many seconds a pattern of conversational gesturing stays active and animated, unlike such relatively short-lived actions as a clenched fist, the obscene flip of "the bird," or the circular thumb and index finger indicating "okay." (These iconic and culturally specific gestures differ fundamentally in duration from the flowing patterns of conversational gesturing.) It is not uncommon for people to simultaneously talk and gesture nonstop for many minutes, especially when speaking energetically. In fact, speaking energetically *requires* gestures that are long, smooth, and loose.

The Impulse to Gesture

When language needs emphasis but emphatic gestures are suppressed (whether by nervousness or a belief that gesture is inappropriate), the instinct surfaces in some peculiar way. It can reveal itself in the twitch of a finger, the flick of a wrist, or a quick flap of a forearm. These are not complete gestures, but an impulse or attempt, revealing that the body is instinctively trying to gesture but is prevented from doing so by self-consciousness or nerves. When you observe these impulses carefully, you can see a direct correlation between the impulse and the words. The impulse is not just a nervous fidget; it shows the connection between speech and gesture in the brain. The hands know instinctively which words are important and need emphasis. The urge to gesture occurs on key words that clarify meaning.

When gestures are inhibited and reduced to twitching fingers and flapping forearms, listeners hear the result in verbal expression. When your gestures are restrained, your speech tends towards monotone. Ideas are not delivered clearly and emphatically because the gesture needed to accompany the word is absent or underpowered. Both your language and your listener suffer.

If you have doubts about how strong the impulse to gesture is, consider how often people plunge their hands into their pockets while speaking. Even tucked deep within, the hands don't stay still. They jingle change and continue to fidget. Look carefully at such speakers, and you can see the impulse to gesture transformed, spasming inside their pockets. The impulse to gesture doesn't go away—it is merely displaced, at times to the detriment of both message and speaker.

To sum up: when you begin to speak, make your initial gestures loose and smooth. Why do we say "She is so smooth!" to compliment a good speaker? Because it is literally true. Natural gestures are larger and longer than the constrained, short gestures of nervous speakers. They are also smooth instead of jerky, slow instead of fast. Given the interrelationship between gesturing, speaking, and thinking, being literally smooth with your arms and hands will bring smoothness to your verbal delivery and mental flow.

What Do You Do with Your Hands When You Are Not Gesturing?

No one gestures all the time, not even avid gesticulators. Gestural flow alternates between action, when hands are moving, and stillness, when they are not. Your hands need a neutral position of readiness that can be used as part of your physical ritual checklist. Before you speak, if your hands are in a position where they are poised to gesture, your gestures will flow naturally.

The Ready Position

The concept of a ready position comes from watching experienced, confident presenters in action, and asking the question, "Where do they put their hands when they are *not* gesturing?" The answer: loosely touching at waist height. Hands and forearms are energized and ready to go, not pressed against the abdomen. The position is loose, not tight. A little bit of space separates the forearms from the abdomen. Consider the logic of this position. In the ready position, the muscles of your upper arm hold a small amount of tension to keep the hands at waist height. Without that muscular tension, the hands drop below the waist to the classic "fig leaf " position, where they are placed modestly in front of the crotch. The fig leaf is the default, unready position of the nervous speaker. While the fig leaf is a perfectly common resting position if waiting for an elevator or the ATM machine, this below-the-waist position leaves the arms and hands under-energized and unready to gesture. The instinct to gesture cannot begin to flow easily when the arms are hanging limply.

Other resting positions that prevent gestures from flowing are the reverse fig leaf (hands clasped behind the back, or what the military calls "parade rest"), hands resting on the lectern, or leaning on a table. The ready position works because it places the hands in the same location where they do most of their work: in front of the body at waist height and poised for action.

Recall where your hands are when you hold and read a book—directly in front of the middle of your body. That is the same general location where arms and hands eat, read, write, compute, text, or check your cell phone. To gesture naturally, start with your hands where they spend the greatest amount of time working.

For most people, the ready position puts hands right in front of the belly button, with biceps slightly energized and elbows bent at ninety degrees. Here, they are also right at the bottom of the zone of gesture that extends vertically from waist to nose. By placing your hands in this position before you speak, and returning to it when you are not gesturing, you will find it easier to trigger your instinct to gesture.

The ready position is virtually "invisible" to your audience. Here's the proof of this surprising observation.

The "Invisible" Ready Position

When lecturing, we routinely say to our audience, "I've now been speaking to you for forty minutes. Raise your hand if you have noticed where I put my hands when I am not gesturing." How many hands go up? Often none at all, sometimes a few. It's a strange thing, but the ready position is invisible to most observers. This is true despite the fact that the speaker's hands in the ready position are precisely at the eye level of the listeners. Why then, is it virtually invisible?

Listeners focus on eyes, not hands. So you can trust that your ready position—hands loosely touching in front of the belly button—will not be consciously seen by those listening to you. It's invisible. Pay close attention to all sorts of speakers and you will see it constantly—the local weatherman, talk show hosts, the TV news reporter from the war zone. They all use it; you've just never noticed. See now what has been invisible to you before.

Never Say Never

Should you *never* place your hands in pockets, behind your back, in the fig leaf? Never say *never*. All those positions are viable options to be used occasionally. The question is—when? If you briefly place your hands in the fig leaf position, reverse fig leaf, in your pockets or on the lectern, that's okay. But be aware that once your hands retreat to one of these resting positions they will stay there longer than is desirable, because bodies at rest tend to stay at rest. Consciously avoid these resting positions at the beginning of a presentation. However, once you liberate your gestural instinct and get it going, it is perfectly acceptable for the hands to cycle through a wide variety of positions.

Variety is the spice of life and of speaking technique. Listening to a question posed by an audience member, for example, may provide a perfect opportunity for the hands to adopt one of the alternative positions. Just don't start in those resting positions, and don't get stuck there too long!

The Mechanics of Readiness

Your hands can touch each other in a number of ways in the ready position. It doesn't matter how they touch, as long as you can keep them still and don't fidget. Wringing the hands—the cliché of nervousness—is the result of adrenaline energizing the hands to rub each other. Use this energy for gesturing instead. The important thing is that your hands remain still, yet ready for your gestures to be released and begin to flow. Do not rest your forearms snugly against your belly for extended periods of time. That is resting, not readiness.

The point of the ready position is to start gesturing immediately. If you remain in the ready position too long, you will appear to have joined a religious order. Resist your body's impulse to interlace your fingers as if in prayer. You will find it difficult to separate your hands; even a little tension in those interlaced fingers will lock your hands together.

If you are long-waisted or have short arms, have an ample paunch or are pregnant, you may need to adjust your hands and arms higher or lower to suit your body type. Experiment to find a position where your elbows can remain still at 90 degrees, but your hands are open and ready to gesture. Try bringing your fingertips together, touching lightly. If you are pregnant and near full term, choose a ready position before it chooses you, as it did for a lawyer whose hands gently rubbed her burgeoning belly during a speech—providing a charming but slightly embarrassing moment in video review.

The Secret Handshake

One particularly useful ready position is the "secret handshake." It is especially helpful for extremely nervous speakers. To experiment with this position, hold your hands with both palms facing forward and extend the thumb of your right hand out to the side. With your left hand, gently grab your right thumb as if it were the handlebar of a bicycle. Pull your hands loosely toward your belly button, and position your hands so that you conceal the fact you are holding onto your

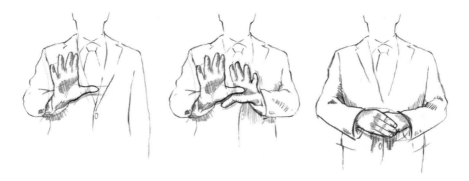

thumb. The secret handshake gives you a security blanket—a warm thumb to hold—yet it permits a quick release of that thumb to allow the gestures to flow. It is also far preferable to the common practice of holding a pen.

Don't Hold a Pen

A surprising number of speakers claim to feel more comfortable when they hold a pen while speaking. Why does a slender cylinder of plastic inspire such comfort and confidence? Holding a pen while speaking is illogical. It makes as much sense as holding a microphone while writing. Yet, silly as it is, holding a pen is a widely popular solution to the problem of what to do with your hands.

Obviously, if you really need to write something down (which is highly unlikely while making a speech), pick up your pen and use it, but then put it down. A pen is for writing, not speaking, and if you hold a pen you will inevitably distract the audience with it. You will click it, fondle it, twirl it, and stroke it. Unconsciously you will fidget with the pen, and this will prevent your gestures from flowing. The energy of adrenaline will animate your hands to play with your pen and annoy your listeners.

What is the real reason that lawyers like to hold pens? It puts the hands into the ready position! People hold pens with both hands at waist height. So keep the ready position but get rid of the pen. The same applies to holding anything in your hands—marker pens, a computer remote control, laser pointers, and even eyeglasses. If you need a security blanket to hold onto, try the secret handshake instead. Put everything else down.

Some Gestures are Distracting

Everyone has seen speakers whose gestures are distracting and even annoying. Distracting gestures differ fundamentally from natural gestures that are useful and effective.

Repetitive gestures become monotonous and call attention to themselves. If you use the same gesture over and over, it becomes distracting. Such gestures merely keep beating tedious time in an annoying accompaniment to your verbal delivery. "Baton gestures," as they are called, make the speaker look like the robotic conductor of an inept marching band. Avoid falling into this gestural rut.

Do not point at the audience with your index finger; it looks like you are nagging rather than informing. Also avoid the "thumb puppet," so popular among politicians, where the tip of the thumb sticks up over the index finger of a loose fist. Your credibility will not be enhanced if you look like a politician.

Avoid:

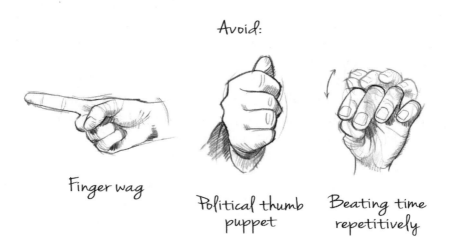

Finger wag

Political thumb puppet

Beating time repetitively

Trust that your natural gestures are not repetitive and monotonous. They are varied because they are inextricably connected to your words.

The Three Rs of Natural Gesture

As you practice gesturing, remind yourself to use the Three Rs: *ready, release,* and *relax.* First, put your hands in the ready position so that they are *ready* to gesture. Assume this ready position before you speak, making it part of your physical ritual of preparation. The second R requires that you *release* your gestures as you begin talking and filling the zone of gesture. Don't wait; gesture immediately. (Specific gestures are discussed in the next section.) As you speak, your hands and arms will be engaged in either *ready* or *release* most of the time. Sometimes for variety and comfort let your arms *relax*—the third R. Take all tension out of your arm muscles so the arms will drop gently to your sides and hang there briefly.

Once you master the three Rs, you can combine *release* and *relax* to give yourself two additional options. While the right hand is gesturing, the left arm can be relaxed and hanging at your side. As the left hand gestures, the right arm relaxes. In other words, don't always gesture with both hands; ambidexterity provides welcome variety. These options—right hand, left hand, and both hands—give you five different ways to use your arms while gesturing. Simply cycle through the five positions randomly, using *release* and *relax* most of the time, but occasionally letting one or both arms relax.

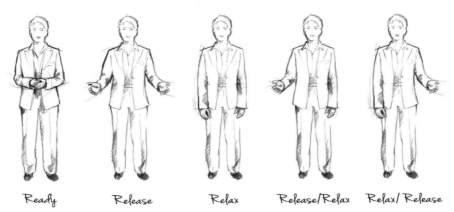

Ready   Release   Relax   Release/Relax   Relax/Release

If you experiment with the ready position and eventually discover that it doesn't work for you, use an alternative. Placing your hands at your sides in the *relax* position can serve as a neutral position when you are not gesturing. This looks fine. Be aware, however, that since the arm muscles are hanging slack, it will take a more conscious effort to start the gestures flowing.

Give, Chop, and Show

Once your hands are placed in the ready position, you will consciously instruct your arms to release an initial gesture. There are three types of gestures commonly used in conversation, and three simple words will help you remember your options: *give, chop,* and *show*. Practice them in private until you can use them with confidence in front of an audience.

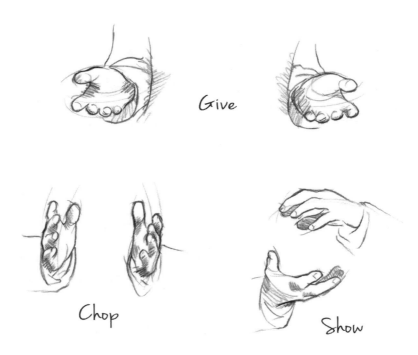

Give

Chop

Show

This illustration is your view:

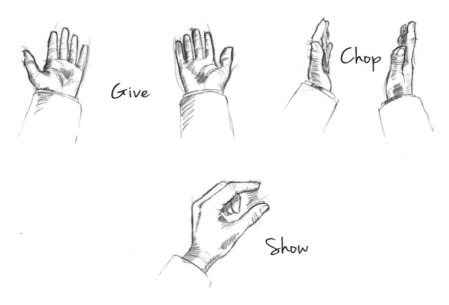

Give. When you give your audience a fact, opinion or rationale, the hand appears to engage in the action of giving. The hand is open with palm facing upwards. Fingers are straightened and separated slightly, neither tensely squashed together nor splayed widely apart. Look at your own hand and do this palm-up gesture now. Use the *give* gesture and say:

The economy is expected to grow at a slow but steady pace.

This gesture can be done with one or both hands.

The *give* gesture is especially useful when combined with asking rhetorical questions of your audience. When used with a question, it becomes the *questioning gesture*:

What lessons can we learn from the last boom and bust in real estate?

You appear to literally hand the question to the audience, just as you would hand a small object placed on your palm. Try the palms-up, questioning gesture with both hands and shrug your shoulders slightly. It is clear you are implying a question even if you don't say a word, for this is universally understood body language.

Chop. When people speak and gesture emphatically, they turn their hands sideways in a gentle karate chop. This is useful when you are speaking more emphatically, trying to get your point across to the listeners. The *chop* gesture accompanies and intensifies a powerful verbal statement. This emphatic *chop* can be done with one or both hands. Hands are usually separated about body-width apart. When the hands are separated even wider than that, the *chop* is big, powerful and authoritatively emphatic. Use the double karate chop to say:

Signing that contract is a big mistake!

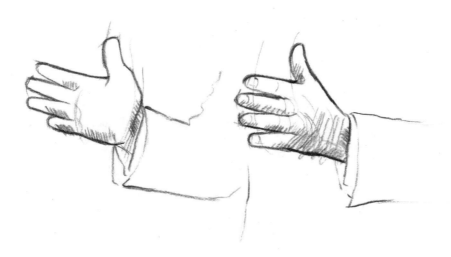

If you find yourself repetitively pointing at the audience, simply convert your pointing finger to the *chop*. Uncurl and straighten the other four fingers. This turns your pointing finger into the chopping hand of emphasis. No one takes offense if all five fingers are pointing together; it is the index finger alone that is bothersome.

Show. The *show* gesture is sometimes a literal enactment of your words. As you speak, the hands recreate the literal action:

His left hand held the wheel and his right hand held his phone.

Like a visual aid, the hands *show* or demonstrate what the words are describing, as in this illustration:

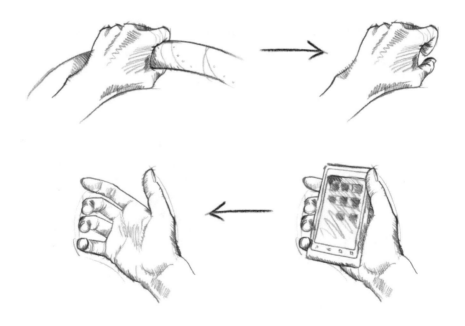

Read that statement aloud and execute the mechanics of the gesture with your own hands to get a feel for this idea. You gesture like this, unconsciously, all the time.

Sometimes the *show* gesture illustrates a concept and functions as a visual aid for the listener. This type of expression is common in conversation:

On the one hand, I'd like to. On the other hand, I'm too busy.

Each gesture *shows* the listener what you are talking about; in this case, contrast between ideas. In conversation the listener might well respond, "I see your dilemma." Gestures literally *show* a visualization that the listener sees. Try it. Use your hands to illustrate issue:

Should we *delay* this project, or *move ahead* with the deal?

Get the feel for *show* with, "The car came within inches of hitting her," as in this illustration:

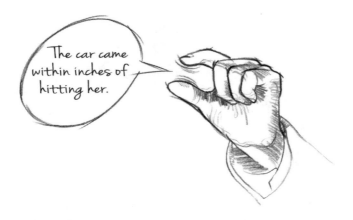

These three choices can trigger your instinct to gesture. Don't be surprised if initially it feels awkward to use *give, chop,* and *show* consciously. It takes practice to get the feel of it. Use the three Rs (*ready, release,* and *relax*) and the three gestures (*give, chop,* and *show*) to simplify the challenge of gesturing consciously.

One last concept completes your gestural vocabulary.

Gesture "On the Shelf"

A useful method for understanding and jump-starting gestures is to imagine placing ideas "on the shelf." The vast majority of natural gestures take place at waist height, and this "shelf" is the bottom of the zone of gesture that extends from waist to nose. Therefore, every time you stand to speak, there is an imaginary invisible shelf in front of you at waist height. When your hands are in the ready position, they are placed on this invisible shelf. It is always there in front of you, demarcating the bottom of your zone of gesture. When you observe conversational gestures, notice that they usually happen at about waist height or on the shelf—even when people are sitting down.

Whether you *give, chop,* and *show,* use the shelf to help jump-start your gestures. For example, asking a rhetorical question of your listeners looks something like the action of placing a big fish on the shelf with both hands.

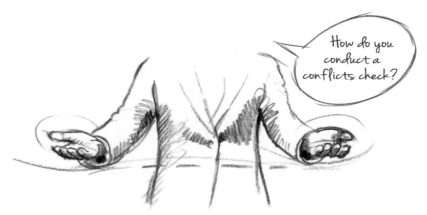

Put the question on the shelf

You can also put the question on the shelf with one hand or the other for variety. Put this book down and try this two-handed *give* gesture right in front of your seated body at about waist height. Then do it with one hand, and then the other. Say aloud and gesture:

How do you conduct a conflicts check?

Make it smooth by extending your hands forward as you say "How," and leave them extended until you say "conflicts check." *Give* the whole question from start to finish.

When using the emphatic *chop* gesture, the invisible shelf is where a martial artist might break a board with a karate chop. Of course, you will not use the *chop* with such violence, but it happens on the waist-height shelf.

Say this aloud, as if you mean it, while using the karate *chop* on the words "not adequately protected."

Finally, the *show* gesture places ideas on this same shelf:

Right now, practice that gesture several times to get the feel of it.

Summing Up Gestures

Your physical ritual prepares you to gesture. As you adopt your stance, center your body, take a conscious breath, and before you speak, place your hands in the ready position. Immediately upon speaking, jump-start your instinct to gesture using *give, chop,* or *show* gestures, and place them on the shelf. Extend your arms so you have some "air in the armpits." Think of your gestures as being slower, smoother, larger, and longer. You now have an answer to the question of what to do with your hands. Practice until it becomes second nature.

Posture and Alignment

Moving up the body, posture is the next topic. What is good posture? *Posture* refers to the position or bearing of the body. We can all conjure in our mind's eye a vision of ideal posture: the body upright and erect, the head held high. Imagine an athlete poised for action, a dancer standing on a stage, or a line of soldiers at ease.

Surprisingly, the conventional wisdom you may have learned about how to achieve this proper posture is wrong. Slouching children are told to put their shoulders back and their chest out. But carrying tension in the shoulders and chest doesn't look or feel good. Instead, you look and feel tense because you are tensing the muscles of your upper torso. It is also difficult to maintain this so-called good posture, because it is downright uncomfortable.

Good posture comes from properly aligning your back, chest, shoulders, neck, and head. Your entire spine—which extends from your tailbone up into your skull—must be aligned to gracefully carry the torso, neck, and head over hips and legs. Good posture includes much more than just your shoulders and chest.

The misguided instruction to pull shoulders back and thrust the chest up is a response to a real and visible problem. Bad posture appears to be caused by the shoulders slouching forward, which makes the chest collapse. But the real problem begins above the shoulders and chest with the incorrect position of the neck and head.

Your Neck and Head

When you think about your own body, do you imagine that the back of your head shares the same plane as the back of your torso? If you could see yourself in profile, chances are that you would discover that your head and neck are positioned forward of your torso. Because you only see the front view of yourself in mirrors, you may be surprised at how far in front of your body you carry your head and neck. (That is, unless you studied ballet for years or have recently served in the military.) People with very poor posture have necks that angle out from the shoulders at 45 degrees, with the head perched way out ahead of the torso. When you watch a crowd of people parade past you, observe this phenomenon. The head leads and the body follows. In contrast, look at very young children; their necks are straight and their heads sit right atop their torsos where they belong.

When your head and neck are too far forward, your shoulders inevitably slouch and your chest collapses. The "shoulders back/chest up" instruction seems to make sense. But collapsed shoulders and chest result from the head and neck being out of alignment. Putting your shoulders back and your chest up does not pull your head and neck back into proper alignment. The best solution is to realign your head and neck so they are properly balanced atop your torso. This repositions your shoulders and chest properly and eliminates tension.

Align Your Spine

Dancers and stage actors are taught to think of good posture as a *direction* to feel and not a *position* to hold. The direction is *upward*, starting from the top of the head. Imagine a flexible bungee cord is attached there. The bungee cord pulls gently upward. As your head pulls up, your neck straightens and lengthens. You neither lift nor tuck your chin as this gentle upward pull occurs. Your face stays on its natural plane, facing forward. When your head and neck move upward, your shoulders and chest move into proper alignment.

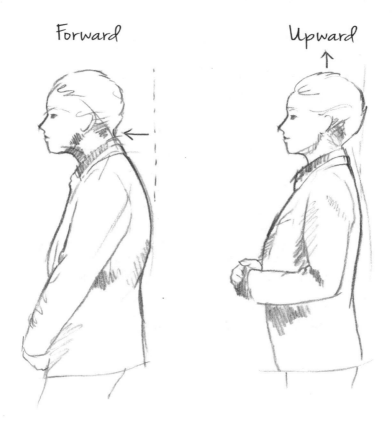

Forward

Upward

You can feel this sensation even while sitting down reading this book. Imagine a gentle force pulling your head upward while lengthening and straightening your neck. Stand up and try it. To find the proper place for your shoulders, raise them up toward your ears and then gently drop them back down. Do this several times to relax your shoulder muscles. You needn't lock your shoulders backward with any tension because your spine can carry the shoulders effortlessly.

Once your head is back on top of—rather than out in front of—your torso, you will look taller and have better posture.

Speaking While Sitting

You will be required to speak sitting down throughout your career, of course. Whether engaged in a group practice meeting, a client meeting, or presenting on a panel in front of microphones, take care that you think about your body position as you sit, just as you do while standing on your feet. Follow these rules:

- Lengthen your spine. Sit up straight and do not slouch.

- Place both feet on the floor.

- Sit on the edge of your seat while speaking.

- Do not lean forward, resting your weight on your elbows.

- Liberate your gestures, and be aware the zone of gesture may be smaller.

- Speak louder rather than lean in toward a microphone.

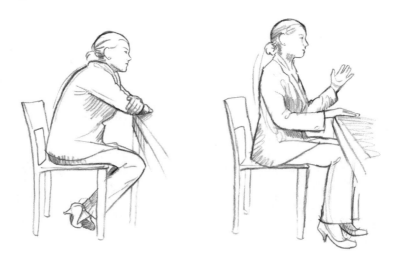

Your physical ritual now includes your feet, legs, breath, arms, shoulders, back, neck, and head. With your head sitting properly atop your spine, let's explore the challenge of making eye contact. Think about faces.

Your Face

People do not notice gestures because they are not looking at hands and arms. They focus instead on faces and, as they listen, most especially on eyes. Because the audience is focused on your face, you must be aware of what it is doing as you speak. Your awareness of your face is based almost exclusively on what you see in the mirror. That reflection of your face is not really how it looks to anyone else; it is a backward mirror image of your face. The left side of your face appears to be the right side and vice versa. Perhaps this is one reason why video is so unnerving. It shows your face as it really appears with the right side on the right side; you aren't used to seeing that image. When you look in a mirror you are not conversing, informing, or presenting. You are passively regarding your face in the mirror. That passivity may lead you to a distorted view of yourself and your natural facial animation.

One of the most frequent comments heard while lawyers watch themselves on video is, "I make all these weird expressions with my face!" But those expressions do not look odd to the rest of the world. The facial animation you may see as unnatural on video is what other people see all the time. As with all elements of physical style, you want your face to do what it naturally does. To achieve this goal, become more aware of your own facial animation and expressions.

Your Mouth

Consider your mouth and lips. It is common for people under pressure to reveal their anxiety by tensing their lips. Some people press the lips tightly together. Others tuck one lip inside and gently chew on it. This tension looks peculiar. Instead, your face should look at ease and comfortable with no visible tension, a look best described as "neutral alert." In neutral alert you appear attentive without revealing obvious emotion; you are neither smiling nor frowning. To achieve neutral alert, part your lips slightly—no more than a quarter of an inch—and breathe through both your mouth and nose. When your lips are slightly parted, they cannot tense, scowl, or tuck.

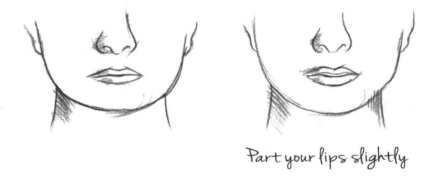

Part your lips slightly

If your mouth naturally turns down in an unintended frown, be especially aware of maintaining neutral alert. Otherwise you may appear to be frowning and scowling at your listeners. Parting the lips slightly makes the frown disappear.

Your Furrowed Brow

Another area of potential tension is the forehead and brow. When people concentrate, they often tense the muscles in the upper part of the face, above and between the eyebrows. This furrowed brow of concentration can make you seem angry and annoyed. Use your physical ritual to become aware of what your forehead is doing. Be sure to include your face and eyes in your mnemonic ritual checklist. Avoid making a scowling, negative first impression on your audience.

Relax your brow

A furrowed brow results from tension in the forehead that draws the eyebrows together. To fix the problem, gently move the muscles in your forehead in opposite directions. When you lift your eyebrows slightly, the tension disappears. Lift your brows whenever you sense that your forehead and brows are tense. Look in a mirror to see this subtle effect. By moving your mouth and your forehead slightly, your face looks alert yet neutral—neither scowling nor artificially happy.

Eye Contact

Everyone knows that eye contact is important. It's as true of personal conversations as it is when speaking to a group. Ultimately, comfort and credibility hinge on the answer to this question: "Can you look me in the eye as you tell me that?" If you don't look your listeners in the eye, you won't be credible.

You must focus your eyes and focus your brain to be able to think effectively on your feet. You can't focus your brain if you don't focus your eyes. This idea is developed further in the chapter about the brain, but it is useful to consider the issue as it affects your eyes.

Even though you *know* you should look people in the eye, making eye contact can be surprisingly difficult when speaking under pressure. There are two reasons for this difficulty. First, everyone has a personal mannerism that dictates where the eyes focus while thinking. Some people think while casting their eyes up to the ceiling; others look at the floor to think, while still others look off to the side. These mannerisms do not need to be eliminated, but they must be controlled. If your eyes flit up to the ceiling as you cast about for the next word or phrase, don't stare at the ceiling for too long. Raise your awareness of your own mannerism and control it. If your eyes break contact briefly, it's not a big problem. But if your eyes appear to linger on the ceiling, floor, or wall for too long, you will look distracted, absent-minded, or simply stumped. The secret to eye contact is to keep returning to focus on people, not things.

Follow this simple rule: never begin speaking until your eyes are focused on another person. Don't say a word until you have lifted your eyes up and out of your notes and focused them on the audience. Resist the powerful temptation to begin speaking while your eyes are still focused on your notes. Talk to people, not paper.

Another factor that makes eye contact challenging is the stoic facial expressions of most listeners. In conversation you get regular subtle feedback from people. They nod, raise their eyebrows, smile, frown, and make those reassuring noises that indicate they are listening. We expect and need some type of physical and/or verbal indication that we are being listened to. Yet when speaking to an audience, almost all of that feedback vanishes.

Stony-faced listeners offer few clues about what they are thinking. If a friend or colleague looked at you with such an indifferent expression you would probably ask, "What's wrong? Why are they looking at me like that?" You may find these passive expressions intimidating and distracting, yet they are natural for people listening to you. It is not their job to telegraph their responses with nods, smiles, or frowns. Thankfully, some listeners may provide limited physical responses, and a speaker's eyes tend to gravitate to those people. But generally listeners sit poker-faced. They may look unfriendly, even hostile. Don't let this throw you. Your job is to make eye contact with all the listeners, no matter how difficult this sometimes may be.

One reason eye contact is challenging has to do with our old friend adrenaline. In his book *Complications: A Surgeon's Notes on an Imperfect*

Science, Dr. Atul Gawande writes about a scientific examination of extreme facial blushing under the pressure of performance:

> *In an odd experiment conducted a couple of years ago, two social psychologists... wired subjects with facial temperature sensors and put them on one side of a one-way mirror. The mirror was then removed to reveal an entire audience staring at them from the other side. Half the time the audience members were wearing dark glasses, and half the time, they were not. Strangely, subjects blushed only when they could see the audience's eyes.*

Psychologists studying the causes of blushing had uncovered a physiological change in the body triggered by eye contact alone. Performance pressure of speaking to audiences triggers adrenaline flow, increases blood pressure, and for some speakers, it causes intense blushing of the face and neck. It is especially apparent at the beginning of a presentation when the audience is most focused on the speaker. But these subjects were not even required to speak; they merely had to stand in silence while being stared at by all those eyes. Eye contact alone increased adrenaline flow, blood pressure, and facial temperature. When the sunglasses blocked eye contact, subjects did not blush.

Being stared at by a group triggers a predator-prey response, and the fight-or-flight response of adrenaline. This physiological response to the gaze of others may help explain why so many speakers find it difficult to sustain eye contact with listeners, even when they know they should.

Despite the physiological challenge of eye contact, you can control where you focus your eyes. Look at listeners individually and repeatedly, even those people with the most unresponsive expressions. Sustained eye contact will enhance your credibility and apparent comfort with them.

Use this simple technique to get your eyes under your control. During those few seconds of silence before you utter a word, look at the perimeter of your audience and make eye contact with the people at the four corners: front row, far right; back row, far right; back row, far left; front row, far left. Within that target area are all the eyes you want to contact. If you stake out the perimeter of your audience, you will help your brain see everyone sitting before you.

How long should you make contact? Here's an analogy for the proper duration of eye contact. Imagine you are watering a garden, and your goal is to water every plant in the garden evenly. You sweep the hose back and forth across the garden plants randomly. You don't want to soak just one plant, washing away the soil from its roots, but to water every plant equally. Similarly, when you look at the audience, look at them all regularly and consistently. You may linger on each pair of eyes for only a second or two, but you can create the feeling that you are talking to them all individually, all the time.

A discussion earlier in this chapter urged you to avoid random pacing. Pacing distracts listeners and requires them to follow meaningless movement around the room. But pacing also robs them of eye contact. One of the liabilities of pacing back and forth in front of your listeners is that you can't make consistent eye contact with everyone. As you move to one side, the folks on the opposite side see your backside and not your eyes. When you move in the opposite direction, the other side is deprived of eye contact. So stand still most of the time and let your eyes move back and forth and up and down, randomly making eye contact.

Eyes and Notes

When you need to look at your notes, don't be afraid to stop and read. Listeners don't mind if you look at your notes occasionally, but they do mind if you talk to your notes. If you stand up and read a script word-for-word, your audience and topic will be very poorly served. (Chapter Two discusses notes in detail.) People don't like to be read to, but they do expect that a speaker will periodically look at notes. So when you do, don't rush. Stop and read. Look down long enough to see where you are and what you want to say next. Then bring your eyes back up, focus on a human being, and begin speaking again.

Summary

To master the challenge of controlling and coordinating your body, you must cope with both your conscious and unconscious behaviors while speaking under pressure. Sometimes you will deliberately jump-start instinctive behaviors such as natural gesturing. Other times your conscious brain helps to prevent unconscious behaviors, such as nervous fidgeting or pacing. Simply telling yourself to be natural will not work.

Adrenaline is a natural source of energy while public speaking, but it can be a nuisance unless you understand and channel it. Be prepared to cope with it each time you make a presentation. Realize that adrenaline can make your legs, arms, hands, and voice tremble. Breathe consciously, using deliberate breathing to control the volume of your voice and to calm yourself. Find and release your own natural instinct to gesture, making sure you have a technique for jump-starting your gestures at the beginning of each presentation. Pay attention to your body's alignment. Release tension in your face, and make eye contact with your listeners.

Develop a physical ritual you will use each time you stand up to speak. Practice your physical ritual until it becomes second nature.

Talk to Yourself

"Take deep, slow breaths while waiting to stand and speak."

"Don't speak until you plant your feet and calmly inhale."

"Look at all of them before speaking to them."

"Part your lips slightly to relax your face."

"Raise your hands to the ready position, and gesture immediately."

"Jump-start gestures and put some opening words on the shelf."

"Gesture slowly and smoothly to start and feel more natural."

"Give away nervousness with the *give* gesture."

CHAPTER TWO

Your Brain

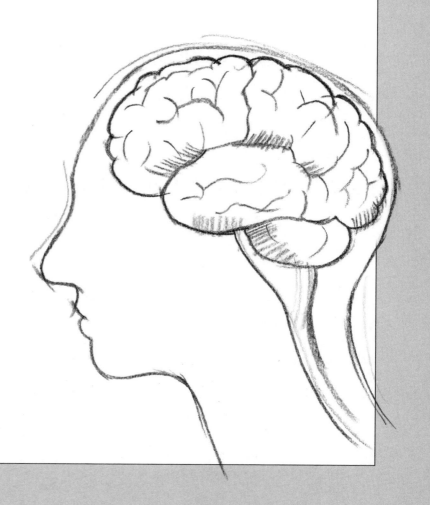

A drenaline profoundly affects your brain as well as your muscles. It is imperative that you understand the impact it has on your cognitive processes, and that you learn how to control and channel its power.

Adrenaline alters how you experience the passage of time. This can help, or hinder, your ability to function as a speaker, as well as your effectiveness in speaking clearly and confidently under pressure. Adrenaline can be an enemy, by making you more nervous and causing you to speak too quickly, or it might befriend you, by creating the sense that you have plenty of time to contemplate what to say.

Most public speakers talk too quickly when nervous. This happens when adrenaline flows to a speaker's brain. It creates the illusion of a time warp; time seems to pass more slowly. To compensate, presenters often accelerate the pace of their speech, but talking too fast only makes thinking much more difficult for both speaker and listener. When you're under pressure, you need extra time to gather and process your thoughts.

Adrenaline and the Time Warp

Induced by a rush of adrenaline, the time warp is a vital complement to the fight-or-flight energy sent to your muscles. When threatened, you must decide whether to stand your ground and fight, or turn on your heels and flee. It would be ideal if you had lots of time to weigh your options and make the right choice when making a life-or-death decision. But you don't have the luxury of time; you must respond instantly to a perceived threat. In this moment of crisis, adrenaline helps you make the right decision by altering your perception of time's passage. It seems to expand the moment, enabling you to weigh your options and make the best choice. You may have experienced this phenomenon if you have ever genuinely feared for your life.

Consider this scenario: You are driving down the street toward an intersection. The light is green. Being a defensive driver, you glance left and then right as you approach to make certain that no vehicle is running the red. Suddenly, there it is! A big green garbage truck is barreling down on the red light, headed for your driver's side door. You've got three seconds to save yourself. You think, *"I'm about to die!"* If you have survived such a moment, you'll recall the feeling of time slowing down. Survivors' accounts of their experiences are consistent: "When I saw that garbage truck, I thought I was going to die! And everything slowed way down." They frequently add: "At that moment, my whole life flashed in front of me!" How, in three seconds, can there be time for your whole life to flash before you? That detailed historical review of your existence occurs as your brain is simultaneously weighing a number of complex alternatives:

Swerve left? No, oncoming traffic!
Swerve right? No, little kids on the sidewalk!
Slam on the brakes? Too late for that!
Speed up? Yes, floor it!

Although scientists cannot fully explain how the time warp works, it's thanks to adrenaline that the brain seemingly has extra time to perform all those complex calculations (involving speed, mass, distance, and even ethics) necessary to assure your safety.

The human experience of time is highly subjective. In everyday life, time appears to pass much faster or slower depending on your circumstances. When you're having fun, time seems to fly by. If you're bored and watching the clock, time slows to a crawl. Of course, the actual passage of time never really changes: a second lasts one second, a minute lasts one minute, an hour takes an hour.

Your subjective experience of time's passage, whether faster or slower, is also influenced by how much information your brain is processing at any given moment. During an adrenaline rush, as you instantly analyze and respond to a perceived threat, your brain processes information at an unusually high rate. In his classic book *On the Experience of Time*, Robert E. Ornstein refers to studies that found "...the amount of mental content in an interval determines its subjective duration." In other words, if your brain is processing increased amounts of information, as it must in a life-or-death situation (or in public speaking), you may subjectively experience time as slowing down.

Another theory involves heart rate and adrenaline. Ornstein refers to a study that showed "…with more 'beats' in an interval, time experience lengthens." Your resting heart rate is about 60 beats per minute. The regular rhythmic tempo of everyday life is *one heartbeat = one second.* Under the influence of adrenaline, however, your heart rate accelerates dramatically to 120 beats per minute or more. Your brain registers twice as many heartbeats per minute, and therefore twice as many "seconds" appear to pass in a given interval.

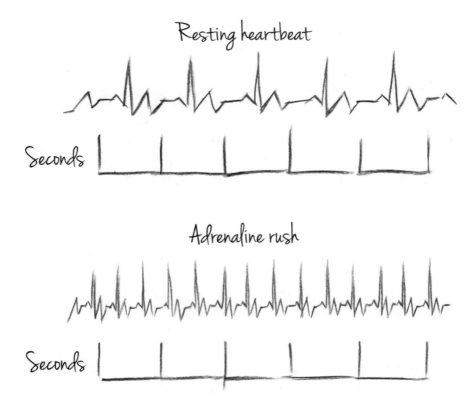

Paradoxically, time seems to slow down as your heart rate speeds up. Does a doubling of your heart rate make time seem to pass twice as slowly? Yes, sometimes. Time perception is idiosyncratic and varies according to circumstance.

While engaged in public speaking, you can turn the subjectivity of time's passing to your advantage. Make it part of your technique; train yourself to channel and exploit the time warp. Rather than allowing it to prompt you to speak faster, use the time warp to give yourself the sense that you have more time to think. Instead of your whole life passing before you, now all available thoughts and words will flash in front of you.

Seeking the Zone of Concentration

Being "pumped," as athletes are in competition, involves both muscles and mind. Muscles are highly energized, the mind sharply focused. Athletes who learn to exploit the benefits of the time warp refer to this heightened state of concentration as being "in the zone." While in this zone of concentration, an athlete has ample time to make decisions concerning the right moves to execute in order to play the game successfully. Tennis legend Roger Federer has described having a leisurely amount of time to return a ball that appears large and slow as it leaves an opponent's racket. Solo climber Peter Croft describes clarity and near-supernatural concentration when scaling a rock face without a rope. For a speaker experiencing the time warp, silence can be particularly uncomfortable and intimidating. Time appears to pass so slowly that a silence of almost any length seems oppressively long, especially at the beginning of a presentation, when the initial adrenaline rush is most intense.

To compensate for these "long" silences, nervous speakers often rush to fill the void with thinking noises—*uh* and *um*—and they talk too fast. This sets a tempo that is impossible to sustain. Talking fast may fill the silence, but it also eliminates your thinking time. As a result, your brain cannot formulate clear, concise sentences or questions. Even if you could speak articulately at a fast pace, your audience couldn't keep up with you. Although your words might be understood, their meaning is not. For the listener, words spoken too quickly go in one ear and out the other. You cannot be clear when your tongue races. Moments of silence are a gift of adrenaline's time warp. Use them.

As it does for athletes in the almost magical zone of concentration, adrenaline's time warp can work for you instead of against you. When you exploit the time warp, your silences will still feel much longer than normal—but in a good and useful way. With practice, the time warp will afford you what feels like an extra long interval to consider what you want to say. Those three seconds of silence feel like twelve. What a luxury to have so much apparent time to think! You've got all the time in the world to choose the right word or formulate your next sentence. You can weigh the merits of expanding upon an example or delving more deeply into a topic. You've got all the time necessary to choose your next word. Silence becomes a valuable tool, an important part of your technique.

Take conscious control of the silence *before* you start to speak. When you first stand up, don't say anything. Pause for a few seconds, and count silently to yourself: one-thousand-one, one-thousand-two, one-thousand-three. It will seem like a long time, but it isn't. Purposefully focus on hearing the silence in the room. Once you've heard it, use it when you speak. Weave short, one-second gaps into your delivery. Say a phrase and stop (silence); say another phrase and stop (silence). At the end of a sentence, and especially at the end of a topic, pause even longer and listen. During that silence—think! You will find that once you begin to focus on silence and its intersection with speech, you grow comfortable using it.

Exploiting the time warp and its partner, silence, enhances your capacity to think and speak effectively. It also increases the audience's capacity to understand and be informed by what you have to say. Silence is a critical component of your listeners' thought processes. They need time to think. If you want to inform, educate or persuade people, you need to give them time to reflect. Listeners require a moment in silence to think about what you just said. The amount of time you take to choose your words is likely the amount of time your listeners need to think about it. Give them time to think and process, and then form an opinion.

Echo Memory

Attentive listeners are using "echo memory." As the word "echo" implies, that is literally what happens in the brain of an attentive listener...

> As you speak... *As you speak...*
> the listener's brain... *the listener's brain...*
> echoes what you say... *echoes what you say.*

Echo memory is used routinely in everyday life. For example, if you hear a phone number, you may simply say it aloud as a memory aid—*555-1212... 555-1212... 555-1212*—until you input the number into your smartphone. That repetition, or echoing, helps the brain remember.

Students taking notes while listening to a professor's lecture are engaged in a version of echo memory. They echo into their laptops or their notebooks the important ideas the professor says. If she speaks too quickly, however, the students are unable to take notes effectively. Whether the listeners are students taking notes or an audience simply taking note of what you are saying, they need time to let your thoughts sink in. The more complex and/or important the information you offer your audience, the more time they need to echo it in their own minds in order to understand and remember it. When you give them time to think about what you say, you are exploiting the conscious use of silence as an element of style. Everyone is familiar with the expression, "Silence is golden." It is derived from a 19th-century proverbial saying—"Speech is silver, but silence is golden"—that emphasizes the key role silence plays in communication. Words are important, silence even more so.

Thinking On Your Feet

Once you realize that you need time (and silence) to think on your feet, the next step is to understand exactly *how* to think on your feet. Should you read? What about memorization? Can you write out what you want to say? What's so boring about simply reading or reciting everything?

Do Not Read

Do not read to the audience from your notes. Reading is deadly. You may be tempted to do so, thinking that it will increase the chance that your delivery will be perfect. But the only perfection you will achieve is to be perfectly boring! It is unlikely that you have been trained, as broadcasters and actors are, to read aloud skillfully. Reading aloud is an art unto itself, and many actors can't even do it well. (Ever watch the Academy Awards? Some film actors can't read a few lines off a teleprompter!)

Everyone makes the same cognitive mistakes when reading aloud. You read too fast. You read without natural expression and inflection, burying your nose in your notes. If you decide to read to your audience, you will rarely look them in the eye, and you will lack credibility. You will sound and look like you are reading—because you are! Listeners are not fooled by reading. If you wish to connect and communicate with people, you mustn't read *at* them, you must talk *to* them.

Do Not Recite

Recitation—repeating aloud or declaiming a text from memory—is a highly specialized skill. Even with years of training and practice, professional actors in a stage play require weeks of rehearsal to memorize and recite their lines accurately and confidently. As a busy lawyer, you can't spend weeks memorizing your presentations. You're apt to have a memory slip—and a single slip can undermine your confidence. If you can't think of the next word to say, you're stumped. Recitation from memory *sounds* odd to listeners. You look a bit glassy-eyed when reciting, since your mind is elsewhere: on the task of recalling what you wrote. So don't try to memorize and recite your presentations; the risk of error is great.

Since you're not going to read and you're not going to recite, you have only one option left. Talk.

Structured Improvisation

The style of thinking for public speaking is best described as structured improvisation. In advance, you structure carefully the order of topics you intend to talk about; then, you improvise word-by-word, just as you do in conversational speech. Your brain is quite adept at this kind of thinking and speaking.

Suppose you say to a colleague, "We need to talk about the meeting yesterday and the seminar tomorrow." Here is your structure:

1. meeting
2. seminar

Using that two-part structure, you simply talk, improvising the words as you go along. As a public speaker, you structure longer presentations with more information; your previous experience with that skill allows you to do it naturally.

Think about a story from your own life that you have told numerous times—a personal anecdote about something humorous, frightening, or bizarre. If you were asked to tell a listener about that experience, you wouldn't hesitate or struggle, because you lived the story and have told it—in effect, have practiced telling it—many times before. Now imagine that you were asked to tell that same anecdote again to a different listener, immediately, but with one additional, impossible requirement: you must tell it verbatim, word-for-word, exactly as you did the first time.

You couldn't do that. Nobody could. This would not indicate that suddenly you were unable to remember the event. It simply would mean that you could not remember and repeat verbatim the words you used to describe it, although you had uttered that description just minutes before. If you cannot accomplish this task even with a familiar anecdote, you can hardly hope to deliver a speech that you wrote in the recent past. The brain isn't built that way.

Telling your personal story requires a form of structured improvisation. The sequence of events is the structure; you improvise around it, retelling the anecdote using different words, phrases, and sentences.

Speaking to an audience using structured improvisation is like performing a kind of verbal jazz. You can learn to be comfortable living in this cognitive state, poised between the opposites of well-planned structure and free-form improvisation. In essence, you train your brain to structure and remember your ideas in a specific order, but not with the precise words you actually will use.

Do Not Read and Talk Simultaneously

Your brain is not experienced at talking and reading simultaneously. In everyday life, when you talk, you talk, and when you read, you read. Do not create notes with prose paragraphs that must be read. Such notes are a trap. The more words you write, the less helpful the notes become. When you are speaking to an audience, there just isn't time to read all those words. If you stand up with a lengthy, detailed script, the temptation to read it will be irresistible. As your brain doesn't naturally talk and read at the same time, it must do one or the other. It chooses reading, because that is the safer choice. But reading inevitably is boring.

The written word is processed in a different part of the brain than the spoken word. Functional magnetic resonance imaging, or fMRI, which can "look" into the thinking brain, reveals that reading and speaking happen in two different areas. To attempt to read your notes while talking at the same time is analogous to running two incompatible software programs on your computer. Your brain's cognitive hard drive will crash. So pick the proper cognitive software: talk to your listeners. Reading aloud isn't effective, talking is. And it is what you already do whenever you communicate.

In dissuading you from reading, we don't mean to suggest that you can't have notes to guide your structured improvisation. Listeners expect that a speaker will look at an outline periodically. It's perfectly okay to *look* at your notes, just don't *talk* to them. There's a huge difference, and it's all a matter of timing. The secret of creating useful notes is to conceive of them as a visual aid for yourself.

Notes as Your Visual Aid

Notes are very often a necessity. In a complicated presentation with lots of detail, notes on a lectern or table guide you through your speech. They help you structure and remember what you want to say, and are a comforting security blanket when your mind goes blank.

Truly useful speaking notes serve as visual aids. Fundamentally they differ in purpose and design from the "thinking notes" you jot down initially as you collect your thoughts about a topic, and are distinct from the "listening notes" you write on your legal pad listening to others speak. Additionally, those thinking and listening notes are not big enough—and often not legible enough—to be a good visual aid for you.

Good visual aids provide a structure around which a speaker can improvise. Here are some rules to help you create good notes for use while speaking.

Write big. If you create notes using your computer, double or triple the size of the font, from 10- or 12-point to 24- or 26-point. Make big notes that are easy to read, so when you glance at them, the words leap off the page. You'll be amazed at how much easier it is to speak with notes you can read easily. They should look something like this:

Write big.

Write legibly.

Keep notes simple.

Keep notes handy.

For handwritten notes, use a pen that makes a fat line on the paper. Big, thick writing can be seen easily, even at a distance. Notes written too small are indecipherable lying on a lectern or table three or four feet away. Consider the distance your eyes are from the page that you are reading. If your notes are lying on a lectern twice the normal distance from your eyes, shouldn't they be written twice as big? If they are lying on a table three times the distance from your eyes, shouldn't they be written at least three times as large as regular writing?

Write legibly. Carefully print your handwritten notes so that they are legible. It takes a bit more time and effort, but it's well worth it. Key words, dates, or dollar amounts might be printed in red to highlight their importance; emphasize important words with a yellow highlighter. When you write legibly as well as large, it prevents you from putting too many words on a page. That's a good thing, because it reinforces the next rule.

Keep notes simple. Less is more. Fewer words are more useful. Boil down your big ideas to just a few words that will trigger the whole thought. Remember, the more words you put on paper, the less useful the notes become. Avoid prose sentences. Write down the structure of your ideas, then improvise around that structure. Don't waste space writing, "Good morning. It's a pleasure to speak to you today. My name is..."

Keep notes handy. Place your notes where you can see them easily. If you are required to speak from behind a lectern, step back about twelve inches—reading your notes should require only a downward shift of your eyes. If you step to the side of the lectern, position yourself so that you can see your notes without moving your feet. Beware of the tendency to step to the side of the lectern, and then forward a step or two. That makes it impossible to read your notes without crab-walking backward to glance at them. Stand *still* where you can see your notes, especially if you need to look at them often.

Horizontal Notes. The notes you create for public speaking will be much more useful once you recognize the difference between how you *write* versus how you think, speak, and gesture. Simply stated: You write *vertically,* but you think and gesture *horizontally.* With this understanding, you can create notes that synchronize with how your brain remembers and how your hands gesture. Ultimately, this even helps your audience understand and remember what you said, which is, after all, your purpose.

When you read and write, thoughts and words flow line-by-line, from top to bottom, down a printed page or a computer screen. Writers explicitly refer to this top-down flow with expressions like, "As described above…," and "…as discussed below." Thinking while reading and writing is about vertical flow from top to bottom.

Thinking while speaking is altogether different. Your ideas and gestures flow back and forth horizontally. This is why using conventional vertical notes for public speaking can be so unhelpful when you are under pressure in front of an audience.

As proof of your own horizontal thinking, consider the expression, "On the one hand…and on the other hand." This gesture pattern is used to compare and contrast, like this:

Does anyone ever gesture such a dilemma top to bottom, vertically?

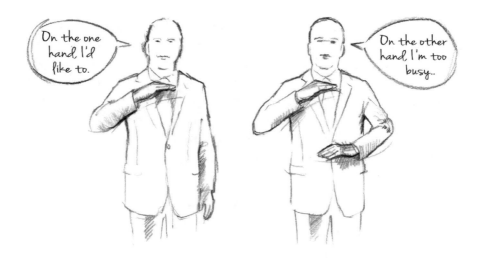

We never do this!

As another example of horizontal thinking, imagine speaking and gesturing about the past, present, and future. How would you logically gesture this personal timeline?

Yesterday I was at work; today I'm at home; tomorrow I leave on vacation.

You gesture the past, present, and future along a horizontal plane. Notice how peculiar it feels to say this sentence aloud while gesturing vertically from top to bottom:

Yesterday I was at work;
today I'm at home;
tomorrow I leave on vacation.

Recall from Chapter One that the horizontal plane where speakers gesture is called "the shelf." When people gesture unconsciously, their hands appear to be placing words, ideas, and concepts on an invisible shelf in front of them. The shelf is about waist high, and speakers appear to use it whether sitting or standing.

If your brain thinks horizontally, and your hands gesture horizontally on the shelf, it makes sense that your notes should reflect this pattern. Create notes that flow from side to side across a piece of paper. Longer legal pads are especially good for this. You can arrange a substantial amount of information across 14 inches of paper. If using your computer, compose and print with the landscape setting. We use horizontal notes while lecturing on the topics described in this book. Here is an example of our horizontal notes:

Body	Brain	Voice
• Adrenaline	• Adrenaline	• Chunking
• Stand	• Time Warp	• Phrasing
• Breathe	• Silence	• Emphasizing
• Gesture	• Thinking	• Gesturing
• Focus	• Echo Memory	• Punctuation

Notice the second advantage of arranging notes horizontally. It forces one to use the characteristics of good visual aids: bigger, simpler, easier to read. Because ideas flow in narrow columns across the page, you must use bullet points and trigger words. This prevents you from writing notes in complete sentences that are less useful during a speech when there is no time to stop and read them.

Imagine you must make a presentation during which you will address a problem, discuss various solutions, and then make recommendations. This illustration lists only the topics on the following examples, leaving out all the detailed bullets:

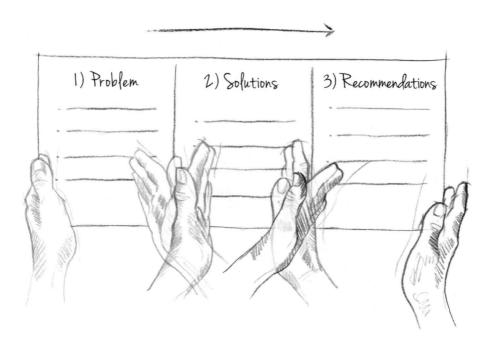

1) Problem	2) Solutions	3) Recommendations

First, you address the problem, next offer various solutions, and finally make recommendations. Your brain tracks along with the horizontal notes, your hands gesture along the shelf using the gentle double karate *chop,* and the audience thinks, "I see what you're talking about."

1) Problem	2) Solutions	3) Recommendations

The way you think, gesture, and make notes all share the same horizontal pattern. And, when you suddenly can't remember your next thought, you know exactly where to look.

If there is one problem with horizontal notes, it has to do with the audience perspective. When your gestures track your own notes from left to right, your ideas appear backwards to your audience, like this:

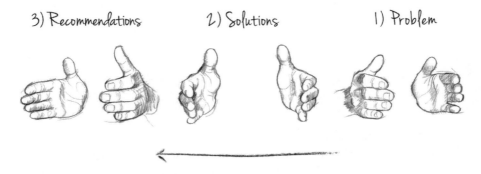

3) Recommendations   2) Solutions   1) Problem

Here is the obvious solution: reverse your horizontal notes and let your gestures follow from right to left. Your audience will see them from left to right.

Consider a presentation about financials for the first quarter. Your notes would look like this:

March	February	January

Your gestures follow your notes across the page:

Your listeners see this:

With some practice this idea becomes second nature. You are doing it for your audience. Simply remember: All patterns start to your right.

Practice using your notes. Speaking with notes is a skill that must be practiced. There is nothing particularly natural about glancing at notes while speaking and making regular eye contact with your audience. Work on it.

Read when you need to. If you need to look carefully at your notes to orient yourself, simply say, "Let's move on." That generic transition line justifies returning to your notes to see what's next in the structure. When you look at the notes, take your time. Listeners know what you are doing, and they aren't bothered by it. They're thinking about what you just said. They don't mind interruptions. Looking at your notes offers them a kind of break, resembling a commercial on TV or radio ("We'll be right back after this short break…"). Once you finish looking at your notes, look at your listeners and speak directly to them. If you do, they'll be patient when you consult your notes.

When you look, *really* look at your notes and read what is written there. Glance backward at the previous topic you just covered. If you forgot to mention something, fix the problem by saying, "Let me back up briefly as I neglected to mention something important about that last topic." In this way, you turn the lemon of forgetting into the lemonade of "something important." Listeners will pay close attention when you tell them it's important. No harm is done. One reason speakers are so glued to their notes is that they are petrified at the prospect of forgetting something important. You needn't be afraid of forgetting. Give yourself time to look over your notes and make sure you have covered everything important in the previous topic before moving on to the next.

Plan to Forget

Many speakers bury their noses in their notes because they're gripped by the fear, "What if I forget?" But that's the wrong question! The proper question to ask and answer is, "*When* I forget, how will I recover?" That you will forget periodically while speaking under pressure is a given. Think how easily you can lose your train of thought when conversing with friends. You pause and confess, "I lost my train of thought. What was I talking about?" If this happens regularly during casual conversation, it's bound to happen during more formal presentations. The obvious solution? Plan to forget. Know that it is going to happen, and be prepared.

As we have suggested, the transitional utterance "Let's move on" can be a useful way to explain and justify your taking a look at your notes and pausing to gather your thoughts. You are moving on, so it makes sense to refer to your notes to see what is next. Or, you can use the same line simply to stop and think. Your audience will understand what you are doing. You have announced that you are moving on, and they see that you are thinking. This is a moment when it is particularly important that you are comfortable with silence. Trust that the audience is watching your cognitive wheels turn. Take the time you need to think about what should come next.

If you are between topics and cannot remember your next area of discussion, simply say aloud the question that is in the forefront of your mind: "What's next?" Having asked that question, look at your notes and find the answer. This is a common storytelling device, especially when telling a story to children:

Then Goldilocks knocked on the door. What happened next, boys and girls? The door slowly swung open.

You can use this same device in your presentation when telling an anecdote or illustrative example:

Then they signed the lease on October 28th. What happened next? On November 3rd the owner of the property...

But what if you can't remember a precise fact, such as a date or dollar amount? One way to deal with that problem is to say:

Now the date the contract was signed [*you suddenly can't remember, so you say*]…

I want to get this exactly right [*and return to consult your notes*]… the date was September 17th.

As you say, "I want to get this exactly right," look purposefully at your notes and check the fact to get it right. The audience sees such careful behavior as an indication of due diligence; it can even boost the speaker's credibility.

The final plan to forget, which may win you some sympathy, is to simply say what you say in conversation, "Excuse me, I lost my train of thought." If it doesn't appear to bother you, it won't bother your listeners. After all, it's natural and happens periodically to them in conversation.

Before you try any of these techniques while speaking to an audience, pause long enough in silence to make sure you really can't remember what you wished to say. The next thought may not quite be on the tip of your tongue, but it is almost certainly somewhere in your brain. Give yourself a moment to find it. Be aware that it is at such moments that the time warp is most oppressive. Don't panic. Take your time. See if the thought is somewhere in your head. Take a breath, and give yourself a moment in silence. If the thought doesn't materialize, act on your plan to forget and use one of the techniques suggested above. If you practice saying these "Plan to Forget" lines before you need them, you will be ready to use them when the moment comes. Say them aloud right now to begin that process:

Let's move on.

What's next?

What happened next?

I want to get this exactly right.

Excuse me, but I've lost my train of thought.

Scripting as a Preliminary Step

Some speakers find it absolutely essential to write out their presentations before creating the final version of their notes. If writing feels like a necessary part of your preparation, don't fight it. But do recognize that writing is only an interim step in the process. For you do not write in the same style in which you speak—in law school you were trained to write like a lawyer, not conversationally. No one really speaks in the language used in legal writings. Even if you had a perfect photographic memory and could stand confidently and recite accurately every word you had written, it wouldn't sound natural. A stilted style loaded with legalese is not very effective when spoken aloud; it sounds too literary and artificial.

However, if writing out your speech helps you organize your thoughts, do it. But then create a visual aid you can easily read, or make horizontal notes. Once you've got a structure on paper, stand up and practice improvising with that structure.

Avoid Thinking Backward

It cannot be emphasized strongly enough that you should *not* try to recite in order to replicate what you wrote word-for-word. If you attempt this, you will find yourself "thinking backward." Your brain cannot simultaneously think backward to what you wrote and forward to what you are trying to say. Your thought process will grind to a halt. Your written presentation is merely one version of your product, and probably not the best version. When you say it aloud the first time, you will use the same structure, but different words to convey it. When you practice it again, yet another set of words will emerge to embody that same structure. Think forward. Describe your ideas with newly minted sentences that will be different each time. The structure remains the same, even as the exact words change. Every time you practice, you will improve by sounding more spontaneous and articulate. To understand how thinking forward can help keep your train of thought on track, consider a concept from cognitive psychology.

Chunking

The human brain prefers to receive information in chunks. If a substantial amount must be recalled, the brain likes to aggregate those many bits of information into chunks so that there are fewer things to remember. Your ten-digit phone number is a good example of this. Because ten numbers are hard to remember, your phone number is divided into three chunks: (555) 123 – 4567. The parentheses and the dash visually break those ten numbers into three chunks that will be easier to remember. Conversely, the brain also prefers for large, complex concepts to be broken up into smaller, more manageable chunks:

1. Problem
2. Solutions
3. Recommendations

Your notes should show the important topics (or chunks) that you will discuss. One way to help your listeners follow your structure is to indicate clearly when a topic or chunk is ending or beginning. The key elements here are *primacy* and *recency*. The brain is more attentive when topics start and stop—at beginnings and endings. People tend to remember the things said first (primacy) as well as the information provided last on a particular topic (recency). Chunking can refer to the macro-level structure of big topics and concepts, but it is also a useful concept for understanding the micro-level of sentence structure. The technique in the next chapter, Your Voice, builds upon this structure.

Structure: Primacy and Recency

Which is a better way to start a presentation, A or B?

A. Good morning. My name is Jeri Cortez, and I'm sure glad to finally be here today, especially after sitting in traffic because of that heavy rain last night and all the road closures. Once we get my PowerPoint presentation to work—not sure what's happening with this frozen screen—I'm sure everything will be, uh, OK. I've got 108 slides to go over in these 90 minutes, so I may have to talk kinda fast. There now, it's working. So. My topic today is ebooks.

B. Why are ebooks the hottest topic in publishing since the Gutenberg Press?

Listeners pay close attention to the beginnings of presentations. Minds often wander in the middle, and retention drops. When the listener gets a signal that the end is near—"In conclusion…"— attention increases once again. Primacy is the first thing listeners hear; recency is the last. Use primacy and recency to structure and remember your presentations. Both you and your audience will benefit.

One reason people listen well at the beginning of presentations is to decide whether it's worthwhile for them to continue to pay close attention. You have a small window of opportunity to capture your listeners' interest, so you must be stylistically and substantively compelling right from the start. If you don't sound as if you care about what you're saying, or are sloppy about your beginning, why should listeners stop checking their email or posting their next Facebook photo?

It will be easier to hold your listeners' attention throughout a presentation if you have grabbed it at the beginning. As the words themselves imply, to *grab* and to *hold* attention takes energy—vocal and physical exertion. As a speaker you must work hard immediately. You cannot afford to warm up slowly and gradually become dynamic, enthusiastic, and interesting several minutes later. If you do that, by the time you've warmed up and achieved a certain level of skill, the listener's mind will have wandered off.

Always begin with a compelling idea, stated as your theme, as in example B. You may then introduce yourself in the second or third sentence. Never ramble on as in A. Do not simply open your mouth and hope for the best. We collect stories of awful beginnings, and are distressed to report that the only time we have ever heard the word "hemorrhoid" in a public speech was in the first sentence of an improvised address to 100 lawyers who had gathered for a two-week program. They were dumbfounded, and doubtless, their minds wandered to unintended ruminations. Similarly, be extremely wary of beginning with a joke. We once sat at a table of extraordinarily accomplished female pilots who endured a joke with the punch line, "I'm afraid this will be the biggest letdown since Elizabeth Taylor burned her bra." None of them laughed.

Even if you begin in a way that immediately captivates the listeners, it is important to recognize that no one listens attentively 100% of the time. Knowing this, your goal as a speaker is to regularly recapture those wandering, inattentive minds in the audience and invite them to pay attention once again. Look at our Attention/Time axis to get a sense of how you can repeatedly refresh primacy and recency during your presentations.

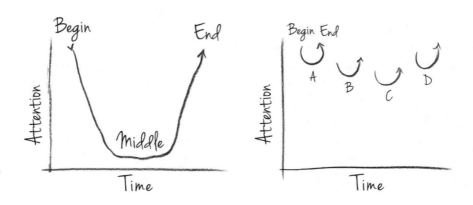

Since beginnings and endings are good, create more of them. Rather than conceive your presentation as having only one beginning and one ending, clearly delineate each topic area. Begin new topics with a headline (begin/primacy) and explicitly mark the conclusion of the topic with a wrap-up (end/recency). When your major ideas are demarcated in this fashion, your presentation will have many beginnings and endings. Each time a new topic is headlined and closed out, the daydreaming (or emailing) listener's attention is refreshed. Here are examples of how to present more topics within a presentation:

Headline: Now that you have listed all the social media sites you want to protect, your next step is to gather all the passwords and put them into a database. We suggest you use Collect 'Em Here.

(In this section you describe where to get the software, how to use it, and how to transmit those passwords securely. Wrap up this topic to emphasize recency.)

Wrap-up: You've got your sites listed, double-checked that you haven't forgotten any, and triple-checked the passwords. What's next?

Or:

Headline: The second topic today is how to make sure your copyrights are filed properly, with special emphasis on the word, "properly."

(Here you define "properly," go over the steps, describe the pitfalls, and then conclude.)

Wrap-up: I cannot overemphasize that you must make sure that every duck is in a row, every "t" crossed, every "i" dotted when filing for e-book copyrights.

Or:

> **Headline:** What's next? You have found three different deeds, all filed with the county, some in conflict with each other. Now you begin the process of making sure you have a Quiet Title.
>
> (Describe the steps, how long it can be expected to take, how much it will cost, and any other important factors.)
>
> **Wrap-up:** Once the judge grants the Quiet Title, your client can shout, "Hooray," and you can move on to the next tasks.

Exploiting the laws of primacy and recency will help you remember the structure of your presentation. Once you have stated aloud to the audience the topic area you are discussing, you will discover it is easier to focus your own thoughts, as well as your listeners', on that one subject. It will assist your memory if you practice saying aloud just the headlines that begin and end topic areas. Once you can make connections between these areas, then you have the structure clear in your mind.

Attitude is a Tactical Choice

There are no boring topics, only boring speakers. If you approach the topic of your presentation with enthusiasm and curiosity, your audience will find it interesting as well. But if you don't bother to choose a point of view, you risk losing your listeners early on. As Marshall McLuhan stated, "The medium is the message." You, as the medium communicating your message, must convey interest and enthusiasm through your tone, demeanor, and attitude. If your topic doesn't appear to interest you, it certainly will not engage your listeners.

For example, if called upon to make a fund-raising appeal for a non-profit organization, you should pick an *appealing* attitude—friendly, positive, open—to accompany your request for funds. If you are nervous, you must convey an attitude that disguises your discomfort. In that case, choose enthusiasm, curiosity, or inquisitiveness. You must choose an attitude before your emotional brain chooses one for you, as it surely will. Your attitude shows on your face and in your body language. Here are some positive, upbeat attitudes to choose from:

compassionate
curious
emphatic
excited
friendly
happy
hopeful
optimistic
polite
surprised
sympathetic
trusting
understanding

And if you are presenting information that is negative, you might choose from these:

apologetic
dignified
contrite
guarded
humble
neutral
pessimistic
regretful
resigned
skeptical
sorry

The most effective way to *appear* and *feel* more comfortable is to behave as if you are. This requires that you select and convey an attitude that is not nervous or anxious, but confident and energetic. Make the attitude you select an integral part of your planning, strategy, and tactics.

Mirror Neurons

A recent discovery of how certain neurons fire in the human brain reveals how important it is—neurologically—to immediately control your body's actions when speaking in public. This revelation begins with a true story about a monkey and a peanut.

The setting is a neuroscience lab in Parma, Italy. A monkey is being used to study a part of the brain that controls movement. His motor cortex is wired in such a way that when he reaches out his hand to pick up a peanut, the action generates a specific sound—*bzzzzzzzz*—through a computer in the lab.

While on a break, his brain still wired, the monkey is sitting in his cage, completely still. A researcher walks into the lab, notices peanuts near the cage, and reaches out his hand to take one. As he does so, the monkey's brain responds—*bzzzzzzzz*—and the computer makes its characteristic "reaching" noise. The monkey doesn't move a muscle, yet the neurons in his motor cortex mirror the action of the person he is watching, triggering the signal as if he had moved.

The researchers are astounded! This incident reveals what are now called "mirror neurons." They exist in the brains of monkeys and humans. One could sum up the discovery of mirror neurons with this rhyme: *Seeing is being, and viewing is doing.*

Our brains mirror other people's actions as we watch them, as if we are performing the action ourselves. Mirror neurons are one of the reasons that human beings are so intuitive about others. We are not just seeing them; we are being them, neurologically. These neurons help explain why watching sports is so compelling, and why fans become emotionally swept up in the action. An athlete's impossible catch or improbable leap is engaging because the fan is not just viewing the action, she is doing it, mirroring an amazing play in her brain. *Viewing is doing.*

This also explains why people cry at sad movies. Accomplished actors trigger our mirror neurons with the "real" emotions we see on their faces and in their bodies, then our mirror neurons communicate with our brains' limbic, or emotional, system. When we watch a well-acted scene in a movie or a play, the actors have connected their actions to our feelings. We have the experience we see.

Similarly, you can exploit the mirror system to inspire feelings of confidence and comfort in yourself and the people watching you. As you stand before an audience speaking, your brain is firing in certain patterns that control your actions. If you could take a simultaneous functional MRI of your brain and those of your listeners, their brains would be mirroring the patterns in yours. Seeing you is like being you. Viewing what you are doing is the same as doing it themselves.

If you act like a nervous person—doing the dance of discomfort with your feet; gesturing with small, fast and jerky motions; letting your eyes dart around the room—your brain fires neurons in nervous patterns. Those same patterns fire in your listeners' mirror neurons, and it makes them uneasy.

Behave comfortably, and make your audience comfortable. Establish immediate control of yourself, and influence how they feel about you. Stand still, breathe mindfully, gesture expansively, and make eye contact. Those actions will calm you down and project confidence and comfort. Your audience will mirror those feelings back at you. That is when you connect genuinely with your audience, making public speaking an exciting and inspiring challenge that you enjoy.

What About PowerPoint?

There is no greater example of the maxim "Less is more!" than Power-Point. Use fewer slides, and fewer words on each slide. The more you write, the less helpful the slides become for you and your listeners.

A typical scenario is this: the first couple of slides are appropriately spare, but by slide three the bullet points have grown into complete sentences. Eventually, the sentences grow into whole paragraphs, and by the presentation's conclusion, the slides are crammed with words from margin to margin.

Don't project your first substantive slide until *after* you have begun your presentation, introduced yourself and your topic, and made a direct, personal connection with your audience. (The split focus demanded of PowerPoint—*Should I watch the screen or the speaker?*—inhibits this essential connection.) Of course, talk to your audience, not the laptop in front of you, or, heaven forbid, the screen behind you. This requires out-loud, on-your-feet practice in using the slides. Warning: just because your slides are legible on your computer doesn't mean they will be legible when projected on a screen.

When we use PowerPoint, we have a presentation of ten slides for a one-hour lecture. We use the slides to show our topics, to assist the audience in memorizing them, and to illustrate a few physical poses. Here are four examples of our slides:

Stand
still.

Gesture
Immediately.

The Zone of Gesture

Stand back
from the lectern.

Make your presentation more interactive with this simple technique: use the PowerPoint slides to pose questions that you will answer aloud. In our lecture, the slide asks this question:

> ## What are the three benefits of breathing consciously?

We lecture about the answers. Sometimes we do the reverse—we ask the question aloud, and the slide provides the answers:

> ## Feel better, speak better, think better.

Your slide might ask, "What changes can we expect?" You then provide the answers aloud. This gives you the security of having your presentation carefully structured by a series of successive questions—"When will the changes occur?" "Who will be affected," etc.—but without your being trapped into having to read each answer verbatim. Or, do the opposite: *You* ask the question aloud—"What are the challenges ahead?"—but let your PowerPoint slides bring up three bullet points providing the answers.

Speaking with PowerPoint slides filled with text is like working off a partial script. You are forced to verbalize each bullet point in sequential order and with words that repeat or closely paraphrase what the text says. That requires you read and talk at the same time, which is difficult for your brain to do. Too many presenters speak to their laptops or screens instead of their audience because they are reading, not talking. Consider this question, therefore, when you use PowerPoint: Are you asking your audience to watch you read your slides, which is deadly boring, or are you talking to your audience, with your slides enhancing the presentation?

Another challenge presented by PowerPoint is that it never tells a story. Yet stories and anecdotes, serving as concrete examples, are what keep audiences interested and make your points memorable. By remembering your story, your listener also calls to mind your concept or point. So, when giving a presentation, periodically say to your audience, "Let me give you an example of that." Then hit the button that makes your screen blank (ideally black), and tell a story or anecdote that illustrates your point. When the story is over, go to the next slide. Variety is the spice of life and communication. Don't feel that everything you say must be repeated by a slide.

Finally, PowerPoint is a must for images that are real visual aids, such as graphs, pie charts, timelines, or photographs. But don't fool yourself into thinking that your outline is a visual aid for your audience. It's only an outline—a structuring device, nothing more. Visual aids are meant to enhance your *audience's* understanding of what you are saying, not prompt *you* on what exactly to say. And if you are asked to provide your audience with a copy of your PowerPoint slides, consider writing a clear summary of your talk in a standard written format and handing that out instead.

Summary

To think on your feet under pressure, you must understand and ultimately exploit the time warp, a phenomenon created by adrenaline that makes time appear to slow down. When you experience this, take your time and don't speak too quickly. Embrace your altered perception and make silence a conscious part of your technique. To get into the zone of concentration, listen to the silence before you speak, then integrate that silence into your presentation, pausing briefly between phrases and sentences. This gives your audience a few moments to think about what you just said. Comprehension happens in the silence, so use it to give listeners time for their echo memory to process your words.

Don't read or recite from memory; get comfortable with structured improvisation. Create notes that help organize your presentation and can serve as a visual aid. Write big, legibly, simply. Practice using your notes, and experiment with making them horizontal. Plan to forget; it's going to happen.

If you need to write out your speech as a preliminary step, do! Reduce your structure to a simple outline or bullet points. Don't try to think "backward" to what you wrote; think forward to what you're trying to say next.

Focus on creating more primacy and recency in your presentations: clearly delineate the beginnings and endings of topic areas. Think and speak in phrases or chunks. Silence is punctuation made audible. Make PowerPoint interactive. Less is more.

Talk to Yourself

"Pick an attitude."

"Hear the silence first, then use it to think while speaking."

"Give them time to echo, so it sinks in."

"Stand back from the lectern to see the notes easily."

"Adrenaline makes time slow down, and gives me time to think."

"Plan to forget, and recover."

"Think forward to what's next, not backward to what I wrote."

CHAPTER THREE

Your Voice

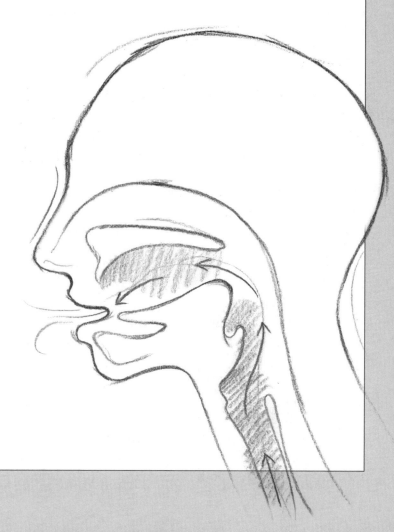

I n everyday conversation, how do you use your voice expressively? How do you adjust your pace, volume, energy, pitch, and tone when talking to different people about various topics?

To become a better public speaker, begin by listening to your own voice in private conversation. You may not be aware of it, but while conversing you continually make adjustments in your delivery. Previously we explored the issue "What do I do with my hands in conversation?" with regard to giving presentations—now ask a similar question about your voice: "What do I do with my voice naturally and expressively when talking with friends and colleagues?" You certainly pay attention to *what* you say in conversation; now pay closer attention to *how* you say it.

Listening to Yourself

Your goal as an articulate attorney is to push beyond what you do naturally with your voice. You need a technique that will give you the vocal power and stamina to speak expressively and audibly for extended periods of time. If you are soft-spoken, you must get comfortable speaking consistently at a greater volume. If you are shy and introverted, you need to become accustomed to being the center of attention. If you talk very fast, you must be able to slow down and control your pace. Most importantly, you should be reliably fluent and articulate every time you speak.

Another challenge is to evaluate your own voice objectively during recorded playback. When you hear your own voice, you probably sound rather odd—to yourself. It's important that you get past this hypercritical, subjective response, as it's unlikely that you sound funny or peculiar to anyone else.

Improving your voice begins with an honest assessment of its current state. To evaluate your voice accurately, it helps to understand why it sounds funny to you on a recording. The answer involves two different ways we hear ourselves speak. When your vocal cords vibrate, those vibrations travel both through the air (to a listener's eardrums or to your own) as well as through your body. You can observe this phenomenon by gently putting your index fingers in both ears and reading these next sentences out loud. Your fingers block the vibrations that normally travel through the air to reach your eardrums. What you hear instead are additional vibrations traveling through the flesh and bone of your neck and skull to your inner ears. Now remove your fingers from your ears, and place the palm of one hand on your upper chest right below your neck. Read this sentence aloud, and notice that as you speak your upper torso also vibrates, which you can feel in your upper chest. This feels particularly intense because your body itself is vibrating, not just the air near your ears.

Without these lower-pitched vibrations conducted by flesh and bone, our own voices on a recording often sound "nasal" to us. However, there's nothing wrong with your voice! Begin to use it with greater power, confidence, and authority. Abandon your self-critical response and tackle the real challenge: using your voice more expressively.

Your Lungs and Diaphragm

Chapter One discussed the necessity and mechanics of breathing consciously. This not only calms you down, it allows more oxygen to reach your brain and enables you to speak with greater power, projection, and control. The muscles that govern respiration include the diaphragm and the intercostal muscles between your ribs. All of these should be warmed up before you begin speaking to an audience.

Observe your breathing as you read this paragraph:

Your autonomic nervous system controls your breath. A small, subtle movement is taking place in your lower torso. Now begin to breathe consciously, and inhale more deeply. Did you notice how much more completely and efficiently you breathed when you fully inflated your lungs? Take an even longer, deeper breath. Work the muscles of respiration more vigorously; push against your belt.

Intercostal Muscles and Your Ribcage

The ability to consciously control your breath is the foundation of mastering your voice. In addition to the diaphragm, the intercostal muscles between your ribs help the lungs expand. Place your hands on the bottom of your ribcage, at the sides of your body about halfway between your waist and armpits. Take a deep breath, and feel the outward movement of the intercostal muscles as your lungs expand. Breathing consciously and deeply creates a three-dimensional expansion: your abdomen moves forward, your ribs push out at the side, and your back extends to the rear.

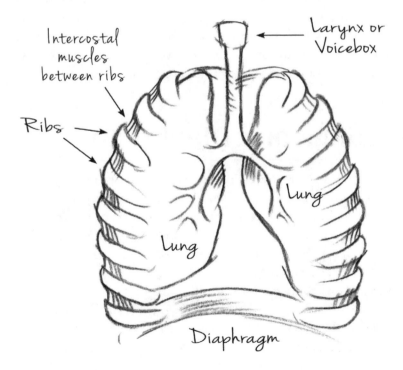

It is important to differentiate between two different kinds of deep breathing. The first is the slow, relaxing breath described in Chapter One. This is the conscious breathing you do prior to standing up to speak. While still sitting down, warm up the muscles of respiration slowly, gently, and carefully. Use deliberate, deep breathing to calm your emotions as well as to prepare to channel the imminent adrenaline buzz. You have time to breathe like this when you pause to look at your notes, walk with purpose in silence to a new location, or simply stop to think. But when you're actually speaking, there isn't time for these slow, measured inhalations; they simply take too long. Although this more vigorous breathing requires you to expend more energy, it replenishes your body with air to support and project your voice.

Project Your Voice with Breath

Recall from Chapter One the advice to breathe in and speak out. Don't misunderstand—this doesn't mean that you should inhale, exhale, and then try to speak. That cannot work, since your lungs would be empty when you needed to speak. Breathe in to fill your lungs, and once they're filled, use the air in your lungs to power your voice.

From the dawn of time until the advent of the microphone, public speakers had to be able to project their voices at great volume. Imagine Caesar addressing the Roman legions, or Lincoln delivering the Gettysburg Address to upwards of fifteen thousand listeners—outdoors and without amplification! When William Jennings Bryan spoke at the Boulder, Colorado Chautauqua in 1900, the local paper reported that his booming voice could be heard a mile away on the University of Colorado campus (the roar was heard, though exact words were not discernible). Those orators had breath control techniques that enabled them to project their voices loudly and for long periods of time.

Today there remain some stage performers with extraordinary breath control and volume. Classical singers and stage actors are still trained to be loud enough to project to the last row of the balcony. Opera singers, in particular, are the Olympians of music-making—the sheer strength of the compressed air in their lungs allows them to be heard over an entire symphony orchestra. Opera singers are often very big people. That extra weight becomes ballast for the remarkable breath support necessary to produce loud, ringing high notes. When they take in a deep, abdominal breath, their extra body weight helps the abdominal wall drop forward, flattening the diaphragm and pulling a large volume of air into the lungs. This air is then compressed by the power of the working abdominals, diaphragm, and intercostals, which push it back up and through the larynx, where the vocal cords vibrate. The length of vocal cords determines voice type and range. Whether a resonant basso profundo or a high tenor, a mellow alto or a dynamic soprano, all big voices are powered by muscle and practice.

This type of muscular breathing has direct applications to public speaking. You may need to fill a large space with your unamplified voice, and be heard by the listeners in the back of the room. Only consistent breath control will make every word audible.

It is natural for your voice to trail off at the end of a sentence as you run short of breath. When listeners cannot understand a speaker, it is often the case that the endings of sentences are too soft. To be loud enough, do what singers and actors do: use your abdominal and rib cage muscles to stay loud—or get louder—as the sentence comes to an end.

Vocal Fatigue

Delivering a long speech sometimes causes vocal fatigue. It's important to understand that the solution for a tired voice lies not in your larynx, but in your abdomen. Your voice tires from a lack of breath support. If there is not enough air passing over your vocal cords, you will add stress and tension to your throat as you attempt to project. This makes you sound worn out and eventually hoarse. If you feel your voice getting tired, focus on your breath support. Work the abdominal muscles more vigorously as you inhale.

Breathe mindfully when pausing briefly between topics. Pause longer between sentences to breathe deeper. Breathing from the belly will save your voice.

Your Larynx and Vocal Cords

Your diaphragm pushes air up and out your lungs so that it flows up your trachea, or windpipe, to your larynx. The larynx is the "voice box" in which your vocal cords are housed. Though sometimes pictured as two thick rubber bands stretched across your larynx, the vocal cords really aren't cords. They are two folds of cartilage attached to the sides of your larynx with a space between them. When you speak, air passes through the folds, causing them to vibrate. The greater the amount of air passing across your vocal cords, the greater the volume (or, in acoustical terms, the decibel level) of your voice. A very soft whisper uses so little air that the cords don't vibrate, while a full-throated shout causes them to vibrate vigorously.

Manipulating your larynx will not increase the volume of your voice. If you add unnecessary tension to your neck, throat, and vocal cords, you will only limit your volume (and possibly damage your vocal cords). Keep your neck and throat relaxed so that air can pass across your vocal cords unimpeded by excess tension. The more open, relaxed, and properly aligned your neck and larynx, the more freely, easily, and vigorously your vocal cords can vibrate.

It's difficult to gain technical control over the vocal cords, since you can't see them. You must rely on physical sensation. Some voice teachers compare the feeling of an open throat to the sensation felt when inhaling quickly and deeply in a gasp of amazement. With your fingers placed gently on your larynx, take in a vigorous inhalation of surprise. Feel how the larynx moves downward as the throat opens. That is the feeling you seek—a relaxed, open throat.

Articulators and Articulation

The articulators—your jaw, lips, and tongue (which interacts with your teeth and the roof of your mouth)—transform a column of vibrating air into intelligible words. Furthermore, your face has 44 different muscles, a large number of which are involved in enunciation and articulation. The more energetically and precisely you work these muscles, the more easily an audience can understand you.

In conversational speech, articulators are often underused, and many syllables and consonants—especially final consonants—are dropped in conversation. Although we write:

Q: When are you going?
A: I'm going to leave about nine.

We often say it using fewer syllables and dropped consonants:

When ya goin'?
I'm gon' leave 'bout nine.

In conversation, the context and melodic contour of a sentence helps people understand each other. Lack of articulation generally isn't a problem. To be understood while making a presentation to a group, however, you must give each consonant its proper enunciation. Taste every consonant. Savor them, even those you may drop in conversation.

Warm Up to Be Articulate

The best way to achieve the clearest speech is to enunciate vigorously, paying attention to the small details of pronunciation. Elocution once was taught to schoolchildren, but now seems quaint. The word evokes visions of an overly formal style, taught by an uptight pedagogue with a starched lace collar and ram-rod straight posture. Actors, singers and broadcasters still study diction, but for the rest of us, the study of declamation and delivery has pretty much gone out of style.

Nevertheless, speaking clearly in order to be understood as a presenter requires precision. Think of your articulators as an important component of your technique. Warm them up before you speak, just as an athlete warms up prior to a competition. Prepare them to go to work immediately, and you are much less likely to trip over your own tongue at the start of your presentation. (Fluency errors early in a presentation have two downsides: they undermine your confidence and can make a negative first impression on your audience.)

Here are a number of ways to warm up. Find a private place and a couple of minutes to stretch and invigorate your articulators and the muscles in your face. If you are now in a private place, stretch the muscles of your face to learn this technique.

Open your mouth as wide as possible; simultaneously, open your eyes and lift your eyebrows. (Don't be shy, no one is watching.) Stick out your tongue as well. Reverse this stretching action by compressing the same muscles. Withdraw your tongue, and scrunch up your face by pursing your lips and squeezing your eyes closed. Now alternate between these two different actions. Stretch and then squeeze, stretch and then squeeze your facial muscles several times. Next, try to move all your facial muscles to the right side of your face, then to the left side. Lift all the facial muscles up, then down. Move your face around at random, stretching every muscle. Now stop, and feel the warm, subtle sensation of increased blood flow in those muscles. Warm up to be articulate right from the start.

Next, warm up the lips and the tip of the tongue. Repeat these nonsense syllables over and over, increasing the speed as you get more comfortable and warmed up:

niminy piminy, niminy piminy, niminy piminy (etc.)

To form the consonant "n," place the tip of your tongue behind your upper front teeth; the "m" and the "p" are formed by the lips. Take a deep breath and exaggerate as you articulate this pattern again. Work the articulators crisply and vigorously, more than you ultimately will use them while speaking. This will prepare you to speak clearly and easily.

Say the same pattern again, this time moving the pitch of your voice from the lower register to the upper register. Move the pitch up and down to warm up your vocal cords as you warm up your articulators.

The next exercise works the articulators from front to back. Say:

butta gutta, butta gutta, butta gutta (etc.)

Say aloud the consonant "b" and feel how it is formed on the lips. "T" is formed with the tongue and teeth. The "guh" sound is formed in the back of your mouth when the back of your tongue arches up to meet the roof of your mouth. Repeat the exercise and feel the shifting of the consonants from your lips to the back of your mouth. Exaggerate and say it again, moving the pitch of your voice from lower to higher to lower to higher.

You also can warm up your articulators by using tongue twisters:

Girl gargoyle, guy gargoyle
Swiss wristwatches

Yet another way to warm up the articulators is to begin a mental list of words that trip your tongue. Collect those words and use them as a warm-up exercise. When you trip over words with consonants that you find personally challenging—perhaps the repeated "s" sounds in the phrase "statistically significant"—use that word or phrase as a warm-up:

statistically significant, statistically significant, statistically significant (etc.)

Say it a number of times, exaggerating the articulation and gradually increasing your speed. Over-articulate these warm-up exercises to increase the blood flow into the muscles of your face and to prepare to speak. Of course, you will not exaggerate your articulation as you speak to an audience, but it is the best way to warm up.

With the muscles of respiration and articulation warmed up and ready to work, the next step is to make choices about how you will channel the energy these muscles provide. To make these choices, you first need to give yourself time to do so, which leads us to a discussion of controlling the pace at which you speak.

Making Expressive Choices

Speech that is articulate, emphatic, and lively requires that you make verbal choices spontaneously. As you select the words to say, you must simultaneously decide which words to emphasize in order to make your meaning clear. To make your point, which sentence deserves extra emphasis?

Within each sentence, which words are most important? Much as you use a yellow highlighter on the printed page, you can use your voice to audibly highlight important words, clauses, and sentences. But it takes time to make these choices. Recall from Chapter Two that adrenaline slows time for you. Use that time—and the silent moments it provides—not only to think about what you are saying, but also how to say it expressively.

Silence is the secret ingredient of eloquent speech. If you are uncomfortable with silence, you will talk too fast; you won't take time to think about what you are saying, and your sentences will be constructed poorly and delivered awkwardly. You will trip over your tongue. You speak first and think second, so your lips move and words are generated before your brain has decided what to say. Also, talking too fast often leads to an excessive use of thinking noises—*uh* and *um* and *y'know*—as the brain struggles to find more time to think. Eventually your self-confidence collapses, and your train of thought threatens to crash and burn. Speaking confidently, on the other hand, begins with controlling the pace at which you talk—and to do so, you must be comfortable with silence. (Recall from Chapter Two that if listeners don't have time to think about what you are saying, they won't remember it, much less be informed or persuaded by it.)

Energy Up, Pace Down

Good public speaking requires more energy than casual conversation. That is why being natural is not enough to get the job done, and why merely being comfortable as a speaker is not synonymous with being convincing. One source of the necessary energy for public speaking is your own adrenaline. It provides the body with extra energy to cope with potentially life-threatening situations. When people are anxious, they often refer to "coping with lots of nervous energy." Co-opt that feeling, and focus on the energy already available within you. Say to yourself, "Good! I'm nervous. That will provide me with extra energy—and energy is the raw material of communicating."

When you think of a speaker with lots of energy, you may suppose that energy and speed are synonymous: an energetic talker is a fast talker. Not necessarily. Energy can be used to speak quickly, but it can also be used to speak emphatically. When people speak dynamically, they use energy for emphasis and clarity, not speed. They become more energetic while simultaneously slowing their pace. The increase in energy signals the importance of what is being said, and the slower pace gives the listener time to think about, and be informed by, what is being said. The energy goes up and the pace goes down.

By warming up and using your breath and articulators, you raise your energy. To slow the pace, employ the concept of chunking. The brain functions best when it has time to formulate language in chunks; likewise, your audience understands better when it receives your message in small bits.

Speak in Phrases, Not Whole Sentences

In everyday conversation, you gather your thoughts into sentences constructed one chunk at a time. Words are grouped into phrases; phrases are arranged into bigger chunks, or sentences. On the written page, punctuation—commas, periods, question marks, exclamation points, dashes—signals a chunk's conclusion. Sentences composed around one idea are grouped into paragraphs, and larger paragraph chunks are delineated visually by indentation and added spacing.

At the very beginning of a presentation, when you most likely are feeling the time warp created by adrenaline, you should consciously speak in phrases and use small gaps of silence between them to think.

The silence between phrases and sentences becomes audible punctuation, signaling to listeners when the chunks begin and end. If there is no silence, there is no audible punctuation. Confusion ensues. Imagine the visual (and cognitive) challenge to a reader if this paragraph were printed as follows, without any punctuation:

> at the very beginning of the presentation when you are most likely feeling the time warp created by adrenaline you should consciously speak in phrases and use small gaps of silence to think between them the silence between phrases and sentences becomes the audible punctuation that gives listeners ears signals about when the chunks begin and end if there is no silence there is no audible punctuation imagine this visual challenge to the reader if the following paragraph were printed with no punctuation at all

All the words are correct, but without proper punctuation it is much harder for the reader to parse and comprehend. Spoken language presents a similar challenge. Listeners need signals—audible punctuation—to mark when chunks start and stop. Whether these chunks are phrases, sentences, or paragraphs, their meaning becomes unambiguously clear through intermittent moments of silence.

Because of the adrenalized time warp, you don't have an accurate sense of what a slow or fast pace really is. Rely on speaking in phrases to give your brain sufficient time to construct each sentence or question carefully, one chunk at a time. Since the brain likes to think in chunks, this strategy fits perfectly with a listener's cognitive processing. This is not the same as speaking slowly in such a way that your creeping pace annoys the listener. Speaking slowly might suggest that you should move your articulators slowly, but that would sound ridiculous. (You... do... not... think... or... speak... one... word... at... a... time.) *Speak in phrases (not whole sentences)* is a more practical instruction for the brain to follow.

If you are a really fast talker with a rapid-fire delivery, control the pace by regularly taking your finger off the metaphorical trigger. Speak in phrases, and in the silence between them allow the audience to digest and be informed by what you have said. Although the words may fly out of your mouth, you still can give the listener time to process those verbal bursts.

Practice saying important sentences at a slower pace to provide contrast. If you say everything at the same quick pace, then it all sounds the same and appears to be of equal importance—and that is never true. To mark their significance, important utterances need to be spoken at a slower, more deliberate pace.

The Mechanics of Phrasing

Imagine the encounter when a parent, unhappy that a teenager has stayed out too late, tells the errant teen not to do that again. The pace slows down; the energy level goes up. Speaking a phrase at a time and maintaining the energy level, the parent says calmly but emphatically:

> If you *ever*
> come home *again*
> *that* late,
> you
> will be *grounded*
> for a *month*.
> Are you *listening*?

Say that out loud, with energy! Say it deliberately, one phrase at a time, and say it like you mean it. Say it like you heard it said to you, or like you yourself have said it.

Use your pace to signal the significance of the message; find a deliberate, speak-in-phrases rhythm that affords abundant time for it to sink in. Do not speak quickly. If this warning were delivered at a fast pace it would not sound as credible, nor be as convincing. In expressive speech, energy is used to emphasize key words; the pace remains slow and deliberate.

We speak in phrases whenever we recite text together as a group. For instance, citizens of the United States are speaking in phrases when they recite the *Pledge of Allegiance*:

I pledge allegiance
to the flag
of the United States of America,
and to the Republic
for which it stands,
one phrase
at a time...

The *Pledge* is a perfect, and familiar, example of speaking in phrases. Use it to set the proper pace at the beginning of every presentation. First, decide what you want to say, and then practice saying it with a deliberate pace modeled on the *Pledge of Allegiance*'s rhythm. Using that rhythm, tell yourself:

That's the rhythm
I can use
to control the pace that I'm speaking.

There are many well-known examples of orators speaking in phrases. In his Inaugural Address, President John F. Kennedy challenged the nation with these words, delivered in chunks, one phrase at a time:

Ask not
what your country
can do for you;
ask what you
can do for your country.

If you recite that quotation aloud but say it quickly, it loses its power. When you say it slowly, and emphasize the key words, you begin to sense the power of speaking a phrase at a time. Say Kennedy's words aloud again, more slowly than before. Hear the short gaps of silence between the phrases. Stretch them even longer. The slower you speak, the more important the idea appears to be.

Vary the Pace

As a public speaker, you will not say everything one phrase at a time, slowly and deliberately. The manner and speed of your phrasing is dictated by the relative importance of what you are saying.

In Chapter Two we discussed that beginnings and endings of presentations should be carefully crafted to take advantage of primacy and recency. Between these beginnings and endings, you'll want to speak in phrases whenever you say something particularly noteworthy, emphasize important facts, or ask important rhetorical questions. You can talk faster when covering preliminary information. A transitional sentence such as, "Now let's explore the potential downside to these proposed changes in policy…", would be a logical place to speak more quickly. The audience doesn't need to hear that transitional sentence a phrase at a time or to concentrate on the preliminary information that follows. You will make choices constantly about how and when to vary your pace to fit your purpose.

Be flexible enough in your pacing to slow down and speak in phrases whenever you come to more crucial points. When you arrive at important information, state it a phrase at a time, slow the pace, and keep the energy high. This gives your listeners time to think about, remember, and be informed by what you are saying.

The necessary variation in pace—slow to fast to slow to fast—is analogous to the movement of a train pulling out of the station. Start speaking slowly to get your train of thought on track. That deliberate pace will signal significance to your audience, when they are paying close attention at the beginning. Inevitably you will speed up as you get going, like a train building a head of steam. Slow down again at each station—each important point along the way—to make certain your listeners are on board.

Since your brain composes sentences a phrase at a time, you are, in a sense, always speaking in phrases. When something is important, the gaps between those phrases become slightly elongated; there is more time, and hence more silence, between them. When you speak more briskly about preliminary or transitional matters, you still speak in phrases, but the gaps between the phrases grow shorter or disappear altogether.

Use Your First Utterances to Set the Pace

Each time you begin a presentation, your first words will set the pace for what follows. Be careful, therefore, about rushing through your first few sentences. Without taking care, it can sound like this:

> Uh, Thank you very much for asking me to speak to the um board of directors this afternoon and I want to give you an overview of.....a list of crucial things....what we've discovered while um examining your company's intellectual property assets and then I'll want to hand out a check list for you and take questions um if there's time.

Attorneys often begin presentations at a fast clip. Smart, well-educated, and accustomed to using complex written language, they often launch a speech with an enthusiasm that can trip them up. When the first utterance is too fast, that hasty tempo tends to persist, and it will prove hard to slow down for the more substantive sections. To avoid this problem, practice the first sentences aloud. Consciously set a slower, more deliberate opening pace. Say it a phrase at a time, rather than tossing it off quickly.

Beware of beginning with the traditional "boilerplate introduction":

> Good morning, my name is Marco Morelli and I'm with the law firm of Morelli & Associates...

You will likely say your name and your firm's name with a speed born of constant repetition, but that fast pace will not serve you or your audience well once you get into the substance of your talk. Use even that boilerplate to set a more measured pace.

Even if you need to introduce yourself to an audience, consider doing so after you have stated the theme of your presentation:

> What can your company do to exploit the intellectual property assets you currently control? My name is Marco Morelli with the firm of Morelli & Associates, and this morning I am here to answer that question.

Consider beginning your presentation with a question that states your topic in interrogative form. This will start your audience thinking, while allowing you to speak with a more measured and controlled pace from the very first sentence. When you begin with a question, the structure of your talk can flow as a series of questions:

> What are those assets?

> How are they currently being used?

> How can you protect them from infringement?

> What's the next step in this process?

Questions facilitate the flow from topic to topic, and are much more interesting than clichéd phrases such as:

> Now I'd like to talk a little bit about the next step in the process.

Begin Sentences Deliberately

Once you are past your boilerplate or introduction and have launched into substance, continue to control the pace. The advantage of speaking more deliberately, one phrase at a time, is that the slower pace, and the additional thinking time between phrases that it affords, gives you greater cognitive control. You literally have more time to consider what you are saying while you say it. If you begin by adopting a delivery punctuated with short, frequent gaps between phrases and sentences, then when one of those gaps is slightly prolonged as you search for a word, it's hardly noticeable. The silences become a kind of insurance against the derailing of your train of thought, enabling you to recover and move ahead. In conversation you begin sentences without knowing how they will end. Use silence to think your way through long, complex sentences without ever stumbling or correcting a word.

Eliminate Thinking Noises

In conversational speech, many people constantly use the thinking noises *uh, um,* or *ah.* This is not an issue of intelligence or education; it's habit. Even highly-educated people tend to use thinking noises far more often than they are aware. And awareness, or a lack thereof, is precisely the problem. Some speakers habitually use 10, 15, or even 20 *ums* per minute! Try counting the *ums* a speaker uses; you'll be surprised by what you hear.

Do you have an *um* habit? Like all habits, this one is subconscious and reflexive, so you may feel no compelling reason to stop—until you hear yourself on a recording. (Listen to a message you've left on voice mail.) It's no wonder that a problem so ingrained through daily repetition is difficult to control. If you know how often you say *um,* you'll be motivated to stop, or at least to reduce its frequency.

Thinking noises are an excellent example of why you simply can't tell yourself to be natural, when being natural may very well include the excessive, annoying *um, uh, like, kind of, sort of,* and *you know* of ordinary conversation. Once you're on your feet addressing an audience, it's too late to begin thinking about eliminating this persistent habit. You must work at changing it far in advance. Make it your goal at work to use no thinking noises at all—not in professional conversation, not in conference rooms, not on the phone or a conference call, and not while talking to clients. Strive to be the always articulate attorney.

Thinking noises typically occur when you speak in phrases but don't use silences as punctuation. In the place of silence, you insert a one-second, monosyllabic *um*. This noise indicates that you know it's your turn to speak but you need a second to think of what to say next. Lasting one second, and occurring on the same musical pitch in the speaker's voice, thinking noises lend a monotone quality to speech that is both distracting and annoying.

Certain words also can function as thinking noises. The expression *you know*, often inserted between phrases and sentences, gives the speaker an additional second to think. Children, teens, and even many adults use the word *like* in the same way. Nothing is *like* a clearer indication that *like* a person hasn't fully acknowledged *like* their professional status than this *like* annoying and childish verbal habit. Summer associates at law firms often are shocked to discover that speaking with this accent of adolescence is *like* highly undesirable. If you talk like a child, people don't take you seriously as a professional.

Another reason that thinking noises are *um* irritating is they intrude on the listener's thinking time. Just when your audience needs a second to consider what you have said, the thinking noise fills the silence like static on a cell phone connection. It interferes with the listener's cognitive processing. *Um* and *uh* are both irritating and counterproductive. Fortunately, they are also completely curable.

Mind the Gap

Passengers in the London Underground system hear an announcement over the public address system whenever a train pulls into the station: "Mind the gap. Mind the gap." A pleasant woman's voice reminds passengers that there is a gap between the platform and the subway car. This phrase, "Mind the gap," is particularly helpful when trying to break the habit of thinking noises. Use it a reminder to insert a gap of silence between phrases. Then follow the instruction: Mind the gap and pay attention! Do you have the urge to insert a thinking noise? Listen to the gap between phrases and sentences. It is a short pause, not a long rumination. During that brief moment, focus your mind on silence.

It is much easier to break a habit when you can give your brain a positive instruction, such as "Mind the gap," rather than a negative one: "Don't say *um!*" The negative instruction doesn't work because it keeps you focused on the problem, not the solution. Rather than tell yourself *not* to do something, encourage yourself to do something *better*. To break verbal habits, focus on the solution and mind the gap.

Remember, any thinking noise you are trying to eliminate is merely an audible indication that your brain needs a second to consider what you are about to say. You are verbalizing your need to stop—for one second—and think before speaking. The solution is to give your brain what it wants—a moment to think—but not to fill the needed silence with a bothersome and meaningless noise. Chapter Four, How to Practice, discusses in detail how to stop saying *um*.

Emphasis and Meaning

Speaking in phrases with plenty of silences helps you project your voice, speak clearly and precisely, compose coherent thoughts, and eliminate thinking noises. Adopting this deliberate pace is also an essential element of speaking articulately to a group. Expressive, powerful speech takes extra time. If you talk too fast, there isn't much time to emphasize key words, which unlock the meaning of speech. Take the time to weigh word choice and expression. The accent you place on operative words can then be shaped to the maximum advantage.

Emphasis is vital for understanding speech. It is the *em*-pha-sis on the right *syl*-la-ble that makes words comprehensible. If someone speaks English with a heavy accent and places the em-*pha*-sis on the wrong syl-*lab*-le, it makes the listener's job more difficult. Intelligibility follows a progression: emphasis on the right syllable makes a word clear, and highlighting operative words makes a sentence understandable. Likewise, the proper emphasis on an important sentence makes a paragraph of thought cohesive, and stressing your most prominent points makes your entire presentation clear. Emphasis gives spoken language a clear and understandable meaning.

Imagine that while describing a commercial deal you spoke the following sentence to the audience: "She never promised the shipment would arrive by Tuesday." The meaning of that sentence will shift in subtle yet significant ways depending on which word you emphasize. Repeat this sentence aloud, emphasizing the key words printed in italics:

She never promised the shipment would arrive by Tuesday.
(maybe *he* did, but *she* didn't)

She *never* promised the shipment would arrive by Tuesday.
(with the stress on *never* it is an absolute denial)

She never *promised* the shipment would arrive by Tuesday.
(you are waffling with the emphasis on this word)

She never promised the *shipment* would arrive by Tuesday.
(maybe she promised the invoice, but not the *shipment*)

She never promised the shipment *would* arrive by Tuesday.
(it could have arrived but shipment wasn't guaranteed)

She never promised the shipment would *arrive* by Tuesday.
(it may have been shipped on Tuesday, but not *arrive*)

She never promised the shipment would arrive by *Tuesday*.
(maybe Wednesday, but not Tuesday)

And finally, one can also emphasize a number of different words in a single sentence:

She *never* promised the *shipment* would *arrive* by *Tuesday*.

This is what expressive, conversational speech sounds like.

An even subtler example of emphasis affecting meaning can be found in a famous quotation from Lincoln's Gettysburg Address:

...government of the people, by the people, and for the people...

That line usually is delivered with the emphasis on the prepositions *of*, *by*, and *for*:

...government *of* the people, *by* the people, and *for* the people...

What happens to the meaning if you shift the emphasis to other words? Filmmaker Ken Burns did just that when directing actor Sam Waterston delivering the *Gettysburg Address* in his documentary, *The Civil War*. Burns believes that the proper emphasis is not on the prepositions but on the people:

...government of the *people*, by the *people*, and for the *people*...

This shift in emphasis changes the meaning. The conspicuous repetition of the word "people" puts the emphasis, both literal and philosophical, in a different place. Say it aloud to get the feel of it.

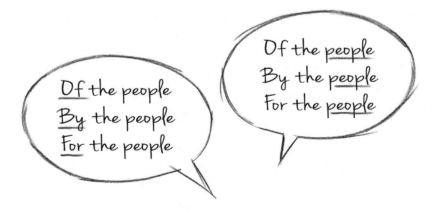

The art of acting rests largely on the power of emphasis to clarify and enrich meaning. The playwright writes the words, and the actor speaks those lines as written. But the actor (together with the director) decides which words to emphasize. In *Death of a Salesman*, playwright Arthur Miller has Linda, wife of the salesman Willie Loman, say of her husband's desperate plight, "Attention must be paid." The playwright doesn't indicate which of those words should be emphasized; the actor must decide.

Attention must be paid.

Attention *must* be paid.

Attention must be *paid*.

Or perhaps every word in that short sentence is worthy of emphasis:

Attention...must...be...paid.

Because acting is an art and not a science, all these choices are possible. Using their trained voices, actors make such choices by the thousands, and these ultimately coalesce into an interpretation of a role.

Public speaking, too, is an art—one in which you must decide which words to highlight in order to convey your intended meaning. But the enormous difference between acting and public speaking is that you do not recite from memory as actors do; you think on your feet. You make extemporaneous choices about emphasis. You do this all the time in conversation without a thought. Virtually every sentence you utter has at least one and often several words that you emphasize instinctively.

Start listening to yourself and to others; hear accent, nuance, and expression in conversation.

Volume, Pitch and Duration

Emphasis can be applied to words by varying volume, pitch, and duration. Often we stress the key words in a sentence by simply saying them louder. Say aloud this phrase from the Gettysburg Address, speaking the italicized words louder:

…government of the *people*, by the *people*, and for the *people*…

Now say it aloud the traditional way, stressing the prepositions:

…government *of* the people, *by* the people, and *for* the people…

Try doing just the opposite with the volume of your voice. Stress the key words by saying them more softly (but still intensely) compared to the other words:

…government *of* the people, *by* the people, and *for* the people…

Emphasis also can be accomplished with pitch. Repeat our example using a higher pitch on the key words. This is the way we usually hear this famous quotation spoken. Now invert the intonation, using a lower pitch on the key words:

…government *of* the people, *by* the people, and *for* the people…

Repeat these words yet again, using first a higher pitch and then a lower pitch to emphasize the italicized words:

…a government of the *people*, by the *people*, and for the *people*…

If you have trouble hearing your own voice navigate the subtleties of pitch variation, make an audio or video recording and listen to yourself.

Emphasis also can be achieved with duration—by elongating the vowel of the accented syllable in the key word. Written language sometimes imitates this practice. Think of the different meanings of these words:

The repeated letter represents a prolongation of the vowel sound. Even in conversational speech, we often emphasize a word by slightly elongating accented vowel sounds. Listen to a recording of "I Have a Dream," Martin Luther King Jr.'s celebrated speech on civil rights. In it, he frequently emphasizes words by stretching their vowels:

> I have a *dream*, that one day this nation will *rise* up and *live* out the *true* meaning of its *creed*: "We hold these *truths* to be *self-evident*: that *all* men are created *equal*."

Say this quotation aloud, slowly and deliberately. Speak it in phrases so that you have the time necessary to elongate the vowels of the words in italics. Then say it again, even slower, and stretch the vowels a bit more. Do you notice how the *pace* at which you speak is related to the *time* you have to be expressive with the words?

Likewise, draw out the vowels of key words in John F. Kennedy's Inaugural Address:

> Ask *not* what your *country* can do for *you*; ask what *you* can do for your *country*.

Say this quotation aloud, speaking it in phrases and emphasizing the key words—especially "you"—by prolonging their vowels.

You can, of course, read these excerpts in two very different ways. You can read the words blandly, with no attempt to capture their inspirational meaning. In such a rendition, every word is given roughly equal weight. Alternatively, you can focus on their meaning by emphasizing key words. Such an emphatic, expressive delivery will allow you to convey the meaning behind the words, and not merely the words themselves. Don't just speak the text; you must speak the *meaning* of those words. Proclaim it, with commitment.

Unlike the orators cited above, you won't write out your presentations in advance and then read them to the audience. You will think on your feet, make choices about the words to use, and decide which ones need extra emphasis and intensity. Communicate by varying the volume, pitch, and duration. You will be living, thinking, and speaking in the present moment—and that's exciting!

When You Must Read

Although reading is usually inconsistent with effective communication, there are times when you must read aloud while making a speech: quoting directly from a statute, Supreme Court opinion, or contract; reading the exact words of the model rules for ethical conduct in a CLE presentation; quoting the exact words of the firm's sexual harassment policy; or reading aloud a quoted text projected onto a screen. When you're obliged to read aloud, read in phrases—slowly. Be aware that your brain, accustomed to reading silently and quickly, will be tempted to read too fast. Read deliberately, a phrase at a time, if you want listeners to fully comprehend the meaning of those words. Adopt a slow, deliberate pace and carefully emphasize key words to express yourself clearly. To achieve this goal, put slash marks in your text to indicate where to break the sentence into phrases, and underline the key words to emphasize.

Ask <u>not</u> || what your <u>country</u> can do for <u>you</u>— || ask what <u>you</u> || can do for your <u>country</u>. ||

You now have an understanding of how to breathe, project your voice, and articulate your words. In addition, you can coordinate your brain and voice by speaking in phrases, minding the gap between phrases and sentences, and emphasizing key words with volume, pitch, and duration to make your meaning clear.

Now, back to gesture! How do your hands help to highlight expressive speech?

Gestures and Emphasis

Your body not only powers and projects your voice with breath from the lungs, it also directs the expressivity of your voice through gestures. The instinct to gesture expressively is connected with the emphatic stress of key words in a sentence or question. As the gesture research of Dr. Jana Iverson has revealed, "…gesturing and speaking are tightly connected in some very fundamental way in our brains."

Look for this connection in your own style. Watch a video of a practice session or a presentation you have made, and look at your hands and listen to your voice. Place a sticky note on the screen so that it hides your face from view, forcing you to focus on your gestures.

Observe that your hands instinctively know which words deserve emphasis. Even when your fingers or wrist reveal only the slightest impulse to gesture, those impulses occur on key words. These impulses are not merely random fidgeting. Your hands know what to do. Trust them.

Gestures, as you'll recall from Chapter One, make you look and feel natural. But perhaps the foremost reason to liberate your instinct to gesture is to help your voice sound natural and expressive. Gesture makes your words and ideas clear and, in the end, articulate and informative or persuasive. Your hands know which words deserve emphasis and which vowels need to be stretched to achieve that. When you don't gesture, your vocal delivery suffers, and so do your listeners. While gesturing has a lot to do with how you look and feel as a speaker, it has an even larger role in how you sound. You could go so far as to say that listeners hear gestures—not the action of the gestures themselves, obviously, but the impact of those gestures on your speech pattern.

Monotone

The absence of gestures leads to an absence of emphasis on key words. Without emphasis on key words, the meaning of all words remains unclear—and you can't be eloquent if your meaning is not clear. Speech with no emphasis on key words slips easily into a difficult-to-listen-to, continuous stream of language stripped of the cues listeners need to grasp meaning. Monotone is literally mono-tonous, taking place all on one musical pitch.

Monotone

Emphasis on key words

Nobody—or more precisely *no body*—speaks in a monotone voice while gesturing. Such dull speech is always devoid of gestures. The next time you must endure an unmusical speaker, transform your suffering into a learning experience. Ask yourself: Is she or he gesturing? Take your eyes off the speaker's face and focus on the hands. You will see that flat speech is linked to a lack of gesture. It follows that one good way to avoid monotony is to speak with your hands and use your gestures.

Conduct Yourself

The speed of your gestures has a direct impact on the pace of your speech. When your hands move quickly, you talk fast. If your hands move slowly and smoothly, your pace slows too. As you speak, use gesture to shape the language in much the same way that an orchestra conductor shapes Mozart or Stravinsky. The speed with which the conductor moves his arms dictates the tempo at which the music is played. The connection between the speed of gesturing and the speed of talking is powerful: it is virtually impossible to speak slowly while gesturing quickly. So if you want to slow the pace at which you speak, gesture more slowly and smoothly. Conduct yourself to control the tempo.

Be Smooth

Smoothness characterizes the gestures and pace of a natural, comfortable speaker. Her movements are not fast and jerky; they are slow and smooth, and her pace of speaking is slower and smoother as a result.

This connection between the speed of gesturing and the pace of speaking is especially important at the very beginning of a presentation. It is important to start gesturing immediately, using movements that are slow, smooth, and expansive. If you do not, your inhibited and restrained initial gestural impulse will lead to small, fast, jerky mini-gestures, which will make you speak too quickly. Your train of thought will be more likely to derail, and you will make a weaker first impression on the audience.

If you begin gesturing at the outset, your natural gestures will make you look and feel comfortable, and will help you speak at a measured and deliberate pace. You will have more time to say carefully what you want to say. Hence you will look, sound, feel, think, and speak more effectively from the beginning. The positive first impression you make will grab the listeners' attention.

The secret of coordinating gestures and words at the proper pace is to practice this complex challenge alone, aloud, and on your feet. Don't leave beginnings to chance and inspiration.

Practice Beginnings with Gestures

Decide, in advance, exactly what you are going to say at the beginning of your presentation. This is one of the few times that you should practice saying verbatim—word-for-word—what you want to say in the first few sentences. Do not trust that on the spur of the moment you will spontaneously say exactly the right thing. It won't happen. (And you leave yourself vulnerable to saying something you regret, as we learned in Chapter Two.)

Once you have found the precise wording of the very first sentences, then think about how to match your gestures to your words and ideas. This coordination, described in the discussion of jump-starting your gestures in Chapter One, involves deciding what words and ideas you will place on the shelf of gesturing. Remember that this invisible, imaginary shelf is where you place your hands in the ready position prior to speaking. Plan logical gestures at the beginning.

You may decide to gesture on the introductory boilerplate. Put your name on the shelf with one hand and your firm on the shelf with the other:

Alternatively, gesture on your first substantive sentence. See how it feels to put two concepts on the shelf. Logically connect your gestures to what you are saying, so they function as a visual aid for the listeners. Emphasizing key words lets your audience see what you're talking about: *economic conditions*, on the one hand, and *new associates*, on the other:

When you end your first substantive sentence with your body in this open and loose position, you send important symbolic messages to your audience as a first impression. The open position of the body says: "Trust me, I'm being open with you. I'm not hiding anything. I'm loose and natural, not uptight and stiff." In addition, you have jump-started your body's instinct to gesture, freeing your brain from any need to worry about what your hands are doing. Think about and practice your initial gestures so that you can quit thinking about them. Instinct will take over when you gesture immediately.

Once you've decided what you intend to say to begin, and which gesture will fit logically with those words, practice coordinating your words with gestures. Thinking about your choice is not sufficient; your muscles need to feel the action. Stand up in a room alone and speak aloud.

Practice so your gestures and your voice have muscle memory. Thinking about gesturing isn't enough; you must practice. (More about muscle memory in Chapter Four.)

There is one more thing you can do to prepare your muscles to gesture immediately and naturally. This mental preparation for physical activity is borrowed from sports psychologists.

Visualize Your Performance

Sports psychologists advise athletes to visualize their actions prior to competing. Athletes practice what they call "mental rehearsal." The Olympic skier imagines the moment when the buzzer sounds and she pushes off to plunge down the mountain in the giant slalom. The sprinter sees the moment when the gun goes off and he explodes out of the starting blocks. As a speaker, you can visualize the initial gestures

you've practiced. Visualizing an action that has been ingrained through practice frees you to gesture with even greater skill and confidence.

Athletes warm up and loosen up physically until right before a competition commences. Sitting in a room about to make a speech, you don't have that same luxury. You may have to sit for a long time before you get to stand up and speak. Even if you warmed up prior to walking into the room, sitting for a long time will cool you down again.

Visualization will help you to be ready when finally you hear the words, "Please welcome our next speaker." As you sit there, think of the words you will say first. See in your mind's eye the gestures you'll use to accompany those words. Hear your pace of speaking in phrases in your mind's ear. Athletes use this visualization technique to win medals; you can use the same technique to win over an audience.

Prosody: The Music of Natural Conversation

Prosody is a general term for the musical elements of everyday speech. It encompasses tempo, rhythm, loudness, silence, and intonation. These musical elements interact with syntax and meaning as you speak. We have examined some musical features already: emphasis on key words lends a natural rhythmic cadence; loudness; and silence. This leaves intonation as the final element of prosody necessary for dynamic speech.

Intonation refers to the up-and-down movement of the musical pitch of your voice. This movement creates the subtle melody of natural speech. We have touched on the dreaded monotone, which lacks all melody or movement. Let's explore the desirable, expressive alternative. No matter whether your voice is naturally pitched higher (soprano or tenor) or lower (alto or bass), you instinctively use a range of musical pitches as you speak, encompassing a lower, middle, and upper register.

To speak well, you need the technical ability to make periodic choices about the intonation and pitch of your voice.

Fortunately, much of the necessary variation of intonation or pitch results from simply emphasizing key words in a phrase or sentence. The very act of emphasis leads your voice to vary the pitch appropriately. That being the case, focus your attention now on the intonation or pitch direction of your voice at the end of a sentence. Whether your voice is descending to a lower pitch or ascending to a higher one as the sentence ends is what creates the necessary "audible punctuation"—the "sound" of a period, question mark, or exclamation mark.

Audible Punctuation

Compare the movement of your voice's pitch at the end of a sentence to going up or down the steps of a staircase. When your voice descends to a lower pitch, it seems to walk down the steps. That is the audible period. When it ascends to a higher pitch, it walks up the steps, the sound of an exclamation mark. When you ask a question, the pitch slides upward, to a question mark.

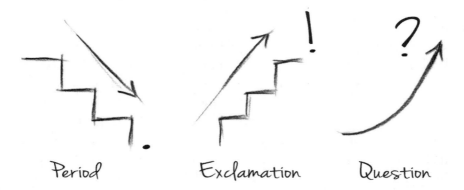

Period   Exclamation   Question

Say aloud these three utterances, using those three different patterns:

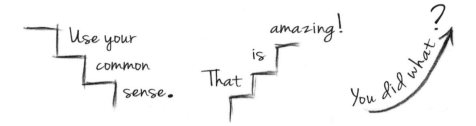

Use the audible period most often, just as you use periods frequently when writing. When you descend to a lower pitch, don't force your voice into an uncomfortable or unnatural range. In a subtle yet significant way, walking down the steps at the end of a sentence conveys confidence and finality. If you expect to convince your audience that you know what you're talking about, you must sound like you believe what you are saying, and say it with confidence. This downward pattern helps to achieve that goal.

The other advantage to walking down the steps is that the finality suggested by the descending pitch buys you some extra time to think about what to say next. Both to your listeners' ears and to your own, that descending pattern signals a conclusion. The sentence is finished. Period. The silence that follows the audible period is like the white space that follows a written period. Your audience has a little extra time to think about what you just said. The sound of finality will help you mind the gap between sentences because this intonation pattern makes the brain less inclined to fill in the gap with a thinking noise.

In addition, this audible period is the way to eliminate the uptalk of adolescence. The repetitive use of the questioning inflection sliding upward at the end of phrases and declarative sentences conveys a lack of certainty, confidence, and maturity. If you wish to be taken seriously, expunge this vocal habit from your speechmaking as well as your professional conversational style. To avoid questioning yourself, walk down the steps.

The audible exclamation mark, or walking up the steps, is useful when you need to add energy to your delivery. It comes in handy during the middle of your presentation if you sense your listeners' attention is lagging. Introduce your next topic and walk up the steps as you do so!

Practicing Verbal Skills

Fortunately, you speak every day of your life, and this affords you abundant opportunities to practice regularly outside the pressurized environment of public speaking. For example, you can practice eliminating thinking noises during a casual conversation with a friend. That is the perfect time to focus some of your attention on eliminating *um* and *uh* as you mind the gap. Do you find yourself regularly stuck in traffic? What an opportunity to practice any of these elements of style (except gestures!). When you find yourself becalmed on the expressway, look at the clock on the dashboard and tell yourself to practice speaking without thinking noises for the next ten minutes. Then hold yourself to that obligation. Talk aloud for a full ten minutes and focus on eliminating thinking noises. When you hear yourself utter an *um* or *uh*, note that it happened, but don't stop and chastise yourself. Correct yourself, and think in silence as you continue.

Brief, regular sessions are more valuable than less-frequent, longer periods of practice time. Since so much of the challenge of speaking effectively is getting started, the more often you practice, the better you'll become at the hard part: the beginning.

You can even practice these speaking skills on the phone. Put a sticky note on your phone that helps you eliminate thinking noises.

Summary

To use your voice expressively, listen to yourself objectively. Get over the notion that you sound funny; you don't.

The power of your voice comes from the muscles of respiration, including the diaphragm and intercostal muscles, working with the abdominal muscles. Clarity of articulation is achieved with the vigorous precision of the articulators: the lips, jaw, and tongue. When you work the muscles of respiration and articulation harder, your listener's job is easier. Stressing the key words in your sentences unlocks the meaning you intend. Emphasis is a function of volume, pitch, and duration.

The music of speech interacts with the meaning of your words. You can exploit this by walking down the steps to sound confident and conclusive. Use the audible period to eliminate the uptick of uncertainty.

Diligently practice the skills outlined in this chapter to savor the power and pleasure inherent in the art of effective and expressive communication.

Talk to Yourself

"Speak in phrases, not whole sentences. Break it into chunks."

"Between phrases, think in silence. It's not as long as it feels."

"Pause after the first phrase to set up a rhythm that works."

"Mind the gap between phrases to avoid thinking noises."

"At least one word in every phrase gets emphasized."

"Gesture immediately and emphasize key words with your hands."

"Avoid the uptick of uncertainty."

"Walk down the steps to end sentences decisively."

CHAPTER FOUR

How to Practice

Practice is the path to expertise. It is the only way to improve skill in any discipline. The more complex the skill, the more practice is required. Whether you want to be a better golfer, pianist, or public speaker, solitary and mindful practice is absolutely essential. You cannot acquire and improve any skill just by thinking, reading, or writing about it. Yet a surprising number of attorneys don't practice—alone and aloud—the skills of public speaking. Practice, while hard work and challenging to fit into a busy lawyer's life, is also a creative act. Once you know how to practice efficiently and effectively, you begin to enjoy it. For some people, practice isn't so much intimidating as it is silly. Others find it downright embarrassing. Yet if you want to be a better presenter, you must overcome any resistance you might feel and learn how to practice.

Practicing is a skill in and of itself—arguably, the ultimate skill. If you know how to practice, you can improve any skill you set your mind—and body—to learning. This chapter will guide you step-by-step through the required skills, and you'll learn to practice smarter, with better results, in less time.

Some attorneys want to believe that adequate preparation for public speaking can occur somehow without practice as the final, culminating step of that preparation. When asked how they prepared for a speech, a surprising number of attorneys confessed that they: 1. read carefully through the relevant material (silently); 2. thought about it; 3. wrote copious notes on a legal pad; and 4. prayed that all their reading, thinking, and writing would somehow coalesce into articulate, expressive speech, on the first attempt and under pressure in front of an audience. Don't put your trust in this self-delusion.

Practice solo, at least at the beginning. Practicing alone, away from the critical eyes and ears of peers, colleagues, or spouses, provides an opportunity to make mistakes in private. It is nearly impossible to say anything well on the first attempt. Everyone needs multiple tries to express ideas well. Solitary practice gives you a chance to rough draft out loud, get ideas flowing, and take risks and make errors when nobody is watching.

Practice must be out loud. The muscles engaged in the motor skill of talking need exercise, just as those involved with breathing and speaking require warming up, blood flow, and conditioning through repetition. Your entire body needs to practice standing still while talking and gesturing. Practice that simulates as closely as possible the way you will speak out loud to an audience should be your goal.

You also should practice a lot—as much as you can. If you are really nervous, only practice will boost your confidence. Even busy professionals can find 10- or 20-minute blocks of time to rehearse. In addition to such individual practice sessions, practice your presentation in front of others, if possible. All practice serves to improve performance.

You must practice alone, aloud, and—ideally—a lot, in order to move ideas that you have read, considered, and written about from inside your head (your neo-cortex) to the tip of your tongue (your articulators). Public speaking is a motor skill.

To Know vs. Know How

There is a critical gap between your brain's capacity to *know* something and your body's ability to *know how* to do it physically. Practice bridges that gap. What your brain knows and understands, your body must practice to execute well. Suppose, for example, you wish to become an expert downhill skier. You read the best book available on the techniques required. Assume, too, that you're blessed with a photographic memory and are able to remember every technique described in the book. By the time you've finished reading the book, your brain *knows* a great deal about skiing. But such *knowing* doesn't mean that your body possesses the *know-how* to tear down a black diamond run. You have to practice what you learned in your reading to develop the physical know-how necessary to swoosh down a mountain like the ski patrol at Telluride. Your body's muscles, controlled by your motor cortex, need to *get the feel* of the required actions.

This chapter will help you practice to develop the requisite know-how. It will help you get the feel of it. To see the results you're hoping for, you *must* practice—because it is your brain that has read this book, not your body. Your body hasn't a clue about the meaning of the words and ideas in this text. To get the feel of it, practice is the only answer.

Practice: Resistance and Avoidance

It's unfortunate that "practice makes perfect" promises an impossible expectation. Forget perfection! Your goal in practicing is much more sensible and achievable: not to make yourself perfect, but to make yourself better. Perfection as a speaker is not only out of reach, it isn't even desirable. The audience doesn't want you to be perfect—they want you to be human, with all the forgivable foibles and imperfections that implies. Your humanity makes you credible.

Practicing with a Mirror

There is a belief that practicing in front of a mirror will help you improve. We find such practice is usually counterproductive, unless you are working on subtleties of attitude and facial demeanor.

The most important reason to practice is to shed your self-consciousness. Mirrors, however, exist precisely to make a viewer more self-conscious, of one's own hair, clothing, or makeup. Since your goal as a public speaker is to be fully aware of your audience—to be able to stand before a group without being overly self-conscious—the last thing you want to do is practice with tools and techniques designed to emphasize self-conscious behaviors. Practice talking to other people, not to yourself. That is virtually impossible if you are staring at yourself in a mirror.

Occasionally, though, using a mirror can help, so here is our suggestion: tape a piece of paper on the mirror so that it obscures your face, but leaves the rest of your body visible. This painless self-decapitation will allow you to focus on your body, and especially on your gestures. As you practice aloud, notice if your gestures are too small or too fast. The mirror now provides immediate feedback without making you excessively self-conscious.

Rationalizations that Inhibit Practicing

"I'm not an actor!"

Some diffident people feel that practicing aloud is synonymous with artifice, pretending, and fakery. Uncomfortable with the self-awareness that practice requires, they worry that their personal integrity and authenticity may somehow be violated. Often they declare, "I'm not an actor! I just can't fake it."

If you are in this group, take a leap of faith. Practicing doesn't make you phony or insincere—it will help you find your natural and authentic self when the pressure is on. When you practice a skill, it becomes second nature, and if you practice enough, it will feel, appear, and be natural.

"I don't want to be over-prepared."

This is another frequently heard rationalization for avoiding practice. What this usually means is that the speaker tried to practice for a short period of time, then felt uncomfortable and quit—and rationalized quitting as a fear of being over-prepared.

"I feel so silly."

There is one very real emotional challenge regarding practicing. Talking aloud in a room when alone is typically taken as a sign of madness! It makes everyone feel, initially, a bit silly, and that feeling may be compounded by the unwarranted fear that someone is listening just outside the door. Frankly, the only solution to this problem is to get over it.

Would you rather feel silly in private or in public? Would you rather feel a bit silly—temporarily—about talking aloud in a room alone, or feel infinitely more foolish by struggling in front of an audience?

Be Patient

Given the challenge of public speaking, be gentle, and generous with yourself as you practice. Be patient. Your progress will be gradual. But if you practice and then seek more opportunities to speak before an audience to put that practice to the test, you will improve.

How to Practice Step-by-Step

When you stand up in a room alone to practice speaking aloud, your goal is to use, develop, and refine the cognitive skill of structured improvisation. Remember: you are not practicing the skill of reading aloud a text you have previously written; you are not practicing the recitation of words you have memorized; you are not practicing in order to memorize your presentation word-for-word so that you can eventually recite it from memory. You will practice extemporaneous speech. You will practice giving your brain an opportunity to process thoughts into words in much the same way you do in everyday conversation, but with one enormous difference: you must be able to think and speak for much longer periods of time, strategically structuring your ideas.

Practice in order to use the same structure, but not the same words, each time. Within the given structure, improvise your words, and vary them slightly. Your brain is fluent at this; now trust that you can do it for longer periods of time while making a presentation.

Before your talk, create horizontal or bullet point notes that detail the structure of your presentation. (Review Chapter Two for suggestions about creating effective notes.) Practice using them.

Practice in the Actual Room

The more familiar you are with the room in which you'll speak, the more comfortable you will be. If possible, get permission to practice in the actual room—and if you can't, try to practice in one that is a similar size. If you are making a presentation at your own law firm, sign out the conference room some evening and practice there.

Visit the room in which you will be speaking, even if you can't practice there. Stand at the front of the room and look at all the seats before you. Sit in the audience, especially in those seats with the worst sightlines in the corners of the room. Bring your visual aids and make certain they are readable by all. If your visual aids can't be read, don't use them.

Run Your Body's Checklist

In your practice room, close the door and gain conscious control of your body before you begin the session. Run your physical checklist, starting with your feet as foundation and moving up the body. The more you practice running this checklist, the more automatic it will become. Eventually your body will align itself before you speak.

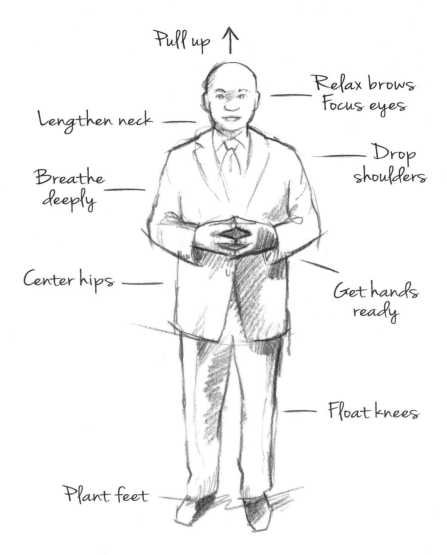

Warm Up Your Voice

Stretch your face very wide and stick out your tongue. Then withdraw your tongue and compress all the facial muscles. Stretch and compress these muscles a few times until you can feel the increased blood flow warming your facial muscles.

Repeat these vocal exercises and tongue twisters, over-articulating and increasing your speed as you go:

niminy piminy, niminy piminy, niminy piminy, niminy piminy, niminy piminy, niminy piminy (etc.)

butta gutta, butta gutta, butta gutta, butta gutta, butta gutta, butta gutta (etc.)

She sells seashells by the seashore

Three free thugs set three thugs free

Statistically significant, statistically significant, statistically significant (etc.)

Speak in Phrases

Begin speaking at a pace that immediately captures the deliberate rhythm used when speaking in phrases. Americans may imitate the rhythm of the *Pledge of Allegiance*. Carefully construct your sentences one phrase at a time to give your brain a chance to collaborate with your speaking voice. Use these first sentences to set a deliberate and manageable pace, just like musicians setting the proper tempo for a piece of music.

Gesture Immediately

Open your hands to gesture just before the first word comes out of your mouth. The flow of your gestures will facilitate the streaming of your thoughts and words. One advantage of starting your presentation with a question—"What are the three big changes in policy that you need to understand?"—is that you can immediately use the palm-up, questioning gesture, with both hands extended toward your imaginary audience. Or place some initial key words on the shelf at waist level:

Jane has explained the *problem*, I want to offer a workable *solution*.

Talk First and Write Second

To help develop a natural fluidity in your presentation style, try talking first and writing second. Let the speech center of your brain generate what you intend to say. Once you've said it, write it down. As you rough draft aloud, stop and jot down the ideas you like best. If you like a particular turn of phrase, add it to your notes so that you can decide later whether to keep it for your final presentation. It can be useful just to free-associate aloud as you begin to shape a presentation.

Rough draft aloud what you intend to say; expect it to be uneven and unpolished at first. There is an advantage to discovering what you do *not* want to say. As with writing, you can go back over the draft to keep polishing it.

Practice Your Beginning

Given the rule of primacy, pay particular attention to the beginning of your topic. Say something that grabs your listeners' attention right at the start, and say it in a compelling way. Make the audience want to pay further attention. Cut to the chase. Have a dynamic purpose from the very beginning. This is as much a matter of sounding as if you have an interesting purpose as it is of actually having one. You don't have to be funny or tell a joke: consider starting with an anecdote that provides a specific and illustrative example of the topic you will be talking about. For example:

> What if you showed up to work one morning, and all your pharmaceutical products were surrounded by yellow police tape? Let's talk about FDA regulatory inspections and how you can avoid such a catastrophe.

Or:

> Is your Facebook account in your will? Is your blog accounted for in your trust? How about Twitter, Google+, and Linkedin? Forget social media hygiene in the present, how will you secure your online assets after you are gone?

Practice Your Ending

To follow the rule of recency, always end your presentations with clarity and confidence, both substantively and stylistically. Practice the ending several times until you are confident that it will put a good finish on your presentation. Avoid the all-too-common non-ending: "Well, I guess I'm out of time. Does anyone have any questions?" If you have practiced your ending, then you can jump to it, even if you run short on time. Use the ending to summarize or reiterate the "take-aways" you want the audience to remember. For example:

> Your checklist for this project can be mercifully short—only three items. First, send your timeline, the one you labored over with diligent care. Second, confirm those dates on the timeline with your contact at the shipping company. Third, stick to the timeline like a dog with a bone. If you never waver, you'll never even come close to getting into hot water.

Or:

> Now we know that the new law looks much more complicated
> than it is, and that it will only affect clients who have failed to file
> this one document. Those few clients will not be happy because
> the fix is time-consuming, but our worksheet makes the process
> relatively smooth. Time-consuming doesn't have to be agonizing.
> A few hours of busy work are much better than years of litigation.

Practice Transitions

As a separate memory exercise, say aloud the transitions that will move
you from topic to topic. The muscle memory of practicing these transitions aloud will help you remember them under pressure. It should be
very clear to you, and therefore easy to remember, why you are logically
flowing from one topic to the next. If the progression isn't clear and
memorable to you, it will not be any clearer to your audience.

While practicing aloud, insert pauses of silence as you transition
from topic to topic. This silence subliminally suggests to the audience,
"Think about that!" To practice being silent during transitions, count
silently to yourself three seconds of silence ("one-thousand-one, one-
thousand-two, one-thousand-three") to let your listeners think about
what you just said. Allow them to contemplate the importance of your
previous topic, then move on. Three seconds will feel like a long time,
but of course it isn't. If you practice counting the seconds silently, you'll
begin to get comfortable with using longer silences for transitions before an audience.

When You Must Read Aloud: Practice!

There are times when you want to read a quotation to an audience.
Practice reading the quote out loud. Resist the temptation to read too
fast for your listeners to comprehend. When you read, here's how to
do it effectively:

1. Pick up the document and hold it up; don't leave it on the lectern.

2. Read it a phrase at a time, emphasizing key words in each phrase.

3. Read the *meaning* of the words, not just the words themselves.

Practice reading aloud slowly and, if you need to, mark up the document to assist your reading. Put slash marks where you intend to pause between phrases, and underline the key words in each phrase that clarify the meaning. A few minutes of mindful practice will ensure that you make the greatest possible impact. After all, the point of reading any document aloud is to have significant impact—don't leave it to chance. If the quote is complicated, don't hesitate to read it a second time saying, "Let me read that again…" and read it even more deliberately and expressively a second time.

When You Recite from Memory

Sometimes the verbatim repetition of a sentence will be useful when quoting a source. Whenever you plan to quote a person or document, however, double-check to make sure you have memorized the text accurately. Practice saying it until you can do so with confidence, and the words roll off your tongue. The ability to quote something precisely from memory can be a very effective tool to use during presentations. For example, you might want to quote a portion of a law, and say:

> The Affordable Care Act states, "A group health plan and a health insurance issuer offering group or individual health insurance coverage may not impose any preexisting exclusion with respect to such plan or coverage."

Break up a long sentence such as this into chunks, like this:

> The Affordable Care Act states
> "A group health plan
> and a health insurance issuer
> offering group or individual health insurance coverage
> may not impose any preexisting exclusion
> with respect to such plan or coverage. "

Next, practice putting these concepts onto the shelf, or use the "on the one hand, on the other hand" gestural template. When practicing a passage that you will recite, use your body as a kinesthetic mnemonic device to help you recall it.

Or perhaps you will repeat a quote from someone, such as this:

> "The Santa Fe County Ethics Board has not received a single report of a suspected ethics violation since the board was created two years ago."

Again, memorize it in chunks, using a gestural template:

> "The Santa Fe County Ethics Board
> has not received a single report
> of a suspected ethics violation
> since the board was created two years ago."

Now you remember that there are four chunks, or phrases, you can see where words repeat ("board" appears two times, "ethics" two times), and it becomes manageable.

Notes and Visual Aids

Once you have structured and practiced your whole presentation, make sure to rehearse with the final version of your notes. Write legibly and large enough so that your notes are easy to see, whether placed on a lectern or left on a table.

If you plan to use visual aids in a presentation, practice working with them. Make sure they're legible for your audience. Sit as far away from them as your listeners will to check for legibility. If you're going to write on a flip chart, practice writing big, legibly, and carefully. Don't rush. Then step back from your writing and see whether it's readable from a distance. Generally, "jumbo" size marker pens make flip chart visuals vastly easier to read than regular markers. Practice using the flat edge of the marker to make the most legible script.

As you practice speaking with your visual aid, stand with your toes pointed toward your imaginary audience. If you point your toes toward the visual aid, you'll end up addressing it instead of the people you want to inform. Pointing your toes toward the audience will keep you facing in the right direction. When you gesture to your visual aid, use the arm that is closest to it. When you point to something on the visual aid, leave your hand there briefly for reference, but turn your head and eyes back to speak to the audience. Touch the visual, turn to the audience, and then talk to them. Think of these as the 3 Ts: touch, turn, talk.

Practice with computer-generated visual aids on a big screen. This will give you a feel for what the audience will be seeing for the first time. Give them time to absorb what is there. When you want your listeners to read what you've put up on the screen, adjust your pace and rhythm to accommodate them. It is counterproductive to ask an audience to split their focus between listening to you and looking at the screen. Tell them what they are looking at:

This is the environmental impact statement.

Tell them where on the screen you want them to look:

Look halfway down the page at the paragraph headed "Brownfield Issues."

Don't talk to the screen; talk to the audience about what is on the screen. If you intend to read from a visual aid, practice reading from it in the same deliberate manner as described above. When you are finished, get rid of the slide by going to a blank that will turn your screen blue or black.

Make a Video

There is no feedback more valuable than seeing and hearing yourself as others do. If you have access to a video camera or a smartphone that makes video, use it. When you practice, don't speak directly at the camera with your eyes focused on the lens—it is too difficult to keep your concentration while talking to a device. Instead, place the camera slightly off to the side, and talk to the whole room.

When you watch yourself on video, avoid harsh self-criticism. Don't focus only on what you don't like, see and hear the positive elements as well. One way to be more objective and technical in your self-analysis is to attend to the observable, quantifiable elements of style: How often do you move your feet? How many steps are you taking per minute? How many seconds do you pause to think or let your audience think? How long does it take for you to use your first gesture? How many seconds do your gestures last? Once you know the numbers, you can set clear goals to walk or shift less often, to pause longer, or to gesture sooner the next time you practice. The Video Self-Review Checklist in Appendix Two will help your evaluation.

Exercises to Solve Specific Problems

"I talk too softly."

If you talk too softly, practice taking deeper, abdominal breaths both before and while you are speaking. Slow your pace deliberately to give yourself time to draw in longer, larger breaths between sentences. Practice speaking a sentence at a time, stopping to take a deeper breath at the ends of sentences. Because emphatic words are louder, accentuate at least one key word in every phrase.

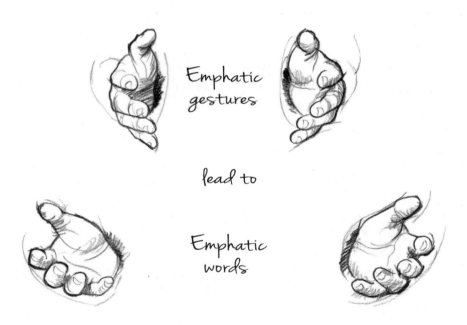

Emphatic gestures

lead to

Emphatic words

Soft-spoken people tend to trail off on the final phrase or word of a sentence. To counter this tendency, speak more loudly as you approach the sentence's end. Deliberately stress the final word of each sentence.

Tell yourself to be louder at the end. This will keep the volume consistent throughout the utterance.

"I just can't stand still."

Stand up and consciously feel the soles of your feet inside your shoes. Wiggle your toes. Feel your feet in contact with the floor, which sits upon the foundation of the building, which is planted on the earth. Your pedestal is the whole planet; feel yourself anchored to it. Do not move your feet as you start to talk. Inhibit the instinct to talk and walk simultaneously. Keep your feet planted as you begin to speak; let your arms do the walking.

Gesture immediately. Although physical energy naturally seeks a path that leads downward, through your legs, send the energy into your arms instead. Once your arms are gesturing properly, your voice will be more expressive too.

At first, practice saying only a single paragraph or topic without moving your feet; gradually, work up to doing an entire presentation standing in one place. Once you can stand still, practice using a limited number of moves as transitions between topics.

"I speak too quickly."

Speaking too quickly is merely a habit, and habits can be broken. Practice speaking in phrases while attending to the short silences separating your phrases and sentences. Before you speak, take a deep breath and concentrate on hearing the silence in the room. When you speak, exploit this silence. Begin speaking, and immediately insert silence between your first phrases. When you come to the end of a sentence, stop for a longer span of time than your instincts might dictate. Imagine that the period at the end of the sentence is a stoplight, and that you plan to sit silently at that stoplight for a short while. Focus less on the speed at which you are talking than on the gaps between phrases when you are *not* talking.

To discover a suitable rhythm, say aloud the phrases below. Hear the silence before and between the phrases:

Your only goal — Silence

while speaking — Silence

is to hear the silence — Silence

between the phrases. — Silence

Use this pace as you practice the various sections of your presentation. Once you can hear the silence, notice how much easier it is to speak when you give yourself time to think. Simply shorten the silent gaps between phrases and sentences until you find the appropriate pace for speaking to an audience. Once you know how to slow yourself down, you can pick up the tempo again.

"My eyes aren't focused."

Make it your ritual to focus first and talk second. Don't speak until your gaze is fixed on an imaginary audience member across the room. Speak aloud as you continue to intentionally focus your eyes. When you find your eyes wandering—perhaps looking toward the floor or ceiling as you pause to think—be aware of breaking eye contact and return to your original point of focus. Look directly at your imaginary audience as you speak. Draw several life-size pairs of eyes on pieces of paper and tape the "eyes" to the wall across the room. Focus on them as you speak.

"I say *um* too much."

To eliminate the *um* habit, substitute silence in its place. Choose a topic that's familiar and ordinary, and begin talking. Describe what you did last weekend. Talk about what you did on your last vacation. Speak at full voice; don't mumble. As you talk aloud, your only goals are to speak in phrases and to mind the gaps between phrases and sentences. The pace isn't important, the silence is. Your aim is to activate your awareness of thinking noises and the silences that will replace them.

Before you begin, hear the silence around you. Start talking, and insert silence into the gaps between phrases and sentences. Here is a typographical example of the pace:

> Last weekend... *(mind the gap)*
> I was extremely busy...*(mind the gap)*
> and I didn't stop for a minute. *(mind the gap)*
> When I awoke on Saturday...*(mind the gap)*
> the first thing I needed to do...*(mind the gap)*
> was to run some errands...*(mind the gap)*
> and pick up my dry cleaning. *(mind the gap)*

Go as slowly as you must in order to keep the silence in the gaps. Become aware of when you use a thinking noise, and begin to hear the preferable, silent alternative.

When you make a thinking noise, hear it and take note of it, but don't stop to chastise yourself. Such a deeply ingrained, persistent habit will continue to appear periodically. Continue speaking, with your goal being to speak for longer and longer stretches without a thinking noise. When you hear one, be mindful of it, and avoid using it as you go forward.

Once you have free-associated about last weekend or your vacation, repeat this exercise but speak about a topic related to the law. Use one that is currently on your mind or on your desk. Explain something legal. Explain the difference between a trademark and a copyright. Imagine yourself teaching a non-lawyer the meaning of a legal concept or term—just as you will need to teach an audience of non-lawyers during a speech. Again, the subject of your talk is less important than your awareness of minding the gaps between phrases.

Keep your practice sessions short; initially, just five to ten minutes is best. Gradually, lengthen the time you are able to speak with articulate control and without thinking noises. Practice longer presentations. Once you have developed sufficient awareness, the next step is to practice conversation without thinking noises. Use silence instead of *um* in more casual settings. The more you do this, the sooner you'll develop a new habit: the habit of speaking without thinking noises. Once you can do this in private conversations, it is relatively easy to be articulate when speaking in more formal, public settings.

Your goal is to be able to turn off the thinking noises whenever it matters. In everyday conversation, *um* and *uh* simply aren't important. Sitting at your kitchen table, talking with a friend in a restaurant, conversing with a colleague at the water cooler—who cares if you say *um* then? You should care, however, about eliminating thinking noises when you are communicating professionally. Whether talking to a colleague or client, in person or on the phone, you should be able to be completely fluent and articulate.

Practice in your office, in meetings, and on the phone.

Informal Practice Sessions

The various practice sessions suggested above are all relatively formal. When you stand up in a room alone to practice aloud, you simulate the reality of public speaking. These practice sessions are essential, but they are by no means your only opportunities to practice. You can also create informal practice sessions to improve your skills. These informal sessions don't allow you to practice every skill simultaneously, but they can be very useful for coordinating your brain and speaking voice.

Here are some suggestions for informal practice:

1. Practice speaking aloud while driving in your car. Although you can't practice gesturing when behind the wheel, drive time offers a good opportunity to practice such verbal skills as eliminating thinking noises, speaking too quickly, or speaking too softly. Discipline yourself to practice for a set amount of time—say, ten minutes. Be uninhibited. If you are driving somewhere to make a presentation, this kind of practice is especially valuable; it serves as your verbal warm-up. Your self-confidence will be much greater if you know that you've already run through your speech a number of times that day.

2. Practice speaking aloud while walking for exercise. You'll be in good company: Abraham Lincoln practiced this way. According to historian Harold Holzer, "To familiarize himself with the speech, he took to reciting passages aloud as he walked down the streets of Springfield…" This is a good time to rough draft aloud your speech. Start by practicing discrete moments, such as the first or the final paragraph. Test out alternative themes this way.

3. Practice speaking aloud during your morning ablutions. As you shower or make coffee on the days you are giving a speech, practice verbalizing aloud what you will say under pressure later. Give your brain and voice a chance to get warmed up and coordinated hours before you must speak. (This type of practice develops muscle memory, which is extremely helpful.) When possible, practice speaking aloud right before you have to perform. Step into an empty room, a deserted stairwell, or even an unoccupied restroom, and say your first sentences aloud. You will be primed and ready to go.

Practice During Everyday Conversations

Every time you speak, you have an opportunity to be articulate and understandable. It is especially easy and useful to practice when you aren't feeling the pressure to perform. In casual chats with friends and colleagues, practice eliminating thinking noises. In personal conversations, slow down your pace and speak in phrases. In meetings or CLE programs, push yourself to ask a question or volunteer an observation as a brief test of your speaking skills under pressure.

Observe, Adapt, Adopt

Steal ideas from good role models. Adapt or adopt some of the elements of their style and make them your own. When you hear truly excellent speakers, look and listen closely to understand why they make such a strong impression. Listen to their pacing. How much do they use silence? Watch their eyes. Look at their gestures. Could you adapt a particularly effective gesture and make it your own? Expanding your gestural vocabulary is like expanding your verbal vocabulary; just as you learn a new word and use it tellingly, you can learn a new gesture and make it part of your personal style.

When you hear mediocre speakers, ask yourself why they make a poor impression. Count the thinking noises. Determine if the pace is too fast. Note those elements of style that you want to avoid in your own delivery, and practice doing the opposite.

The Law of Opposites

As you hone your style, become aware of its individual elements. Perhaps you speak with volume and authority, and are an articulate but fast talker. You gesture regularly as part of emphasizing key words. Simply put, you are loud, fast, and animated. These are all good things to have as elements of your personal style, but it is possible to have too much of a good thing. Contrast and variety will best be achieved if you tell yourself periodically that in addition to being loud, fast, and animated, you can also be softer, slower, and still. Invoke the law of opposites, and allow your loud voice to be softer at times, your fast delivery slower, and your animated gestures still.

When you obey the law of opposites, you suddenly have twice as many skills to call upon. Rather than just playing to your strengths—loud, fast, animated—you also play against them. This keeps your delivery interesting. The audience then anticipates the next surprise and contrast, rather than feeling perpetually barraged by the same stylistic elements. Human beings crave variety. We quickly tire of the same old thing repeated over and over again. This is especially true of style. Surprise your audience and mix up your choices to keep your voice and presentation from becoming predictable, repetitive, and, ultimately, boring.

When you go in an unexpected stylistic direction, you gain a new expressive capacity. Surprising your listener puts emphasis on important words, phrases, sentences, and rhetorical questions. If your style is loud, fast, and animated, you can't highlight important points very well by becoming even louder, faster, and more animated. That would be too much! Instead, choose from a broader range of stylistic elements. Ask yourself, "What is the opposite of my usual demeanor?" Add an exotic spice to a favorite recipe. You need just a dash of soft, slow, and still, not a personality transplant or a radical change of delivery. Rehearse uncharacteristic choices long before you're under the pressure of making a speech. With practice, you will find that your stylistic vocabulary has widened and that you can make novel choices spontaneously. Like a skilled jazz musician, you eventually will live in the present and instinctively feel the moment when a choice is right.

Practicing for the Mental Challenge

Finding your rituals, developing a solid technique, and relying on good speaking habits all go a long way towards helping you feel prepared to stand before an audience. Psyching yourself up for speaking, rather than psyching yourself out, is one last critical part of your technique. You have to play the "head game" successfully if you strive to anticipate and look forward to the pressure of performing as a speaker. Mental preparation for speaking is just as much a matter of technique and practice as are eliminating thinking noises and learning to stand still. Every lawyer faces unique challenges in getting ready.

Remember you are attempting to win over an audience. To play to win, psych yourself up before competing, just as athletes do. Athletes chant, shout, and supportively slap each other to get psyched up. Pump yourself up as part of your technique: "I can do this! I can win them over." Confidence is based on preparation. Tell yourself, "I'm ready. I practiced. I've done everything I can to prepare for this speech." Use the techniques in this book to be prepared. Then, you can psych yourself up, not out. If you have ever had a really unpleasant speaking experience, you may suffer from what we have come to call PTSD or "post-traumatic speaking disorder." Perhaps you blanked while speaking to your peers in law school, college, or even earlier in your life. Does that one bad experience haunt you still? If so, it's time to get over it.

Make a video while practicing and review it using the Video Self-Review Checklist in the Appendix. Watch and listen, focusing on the positive elements of style. On a piece of paper, tally the things you already do that work well. Be specific: "I stand still. I don't say *um*. I gesture naturally. I don't appear nervous." Build your newfound confidence on that foundation.

Don't be overly critical of the things you don't like, or waste negative energy on things you can't change: "I should lose weight." or "My eyes are too close together." That behavior psyches you out. Stop it.

The next time you have to perform, study that list of positive behaviors and tell yourself, "Here's what I do that works." Focus on those positive elements of your style, and you will gradually overcome PTSD, putting it behind you forever. Speaking in public can trigger deeply personal issues and anxieties. Some lawyers confess they hate being the center of attention. Others don't like to be stared at intensely. Still others don't like making eye contact with strangers. If you are dealing with any of these issues, you can change. Make a conscious decision to work on your personal anxiety. Pinpoint what bothers you the most, then practice that specific skill, and get comfortable doing it.

Of all the techniques in this book, the practice of conscious breathing is both the most important and also the most undervalued. As you prepare for a speech, deliberate breathing can help turn off unhelpful thoughts of negative anticipation. When the person introducing you says, "Here's our next speaker!" and you know you are about to begin, breathing is the last thing you can do to keep your wits about you. The more you employ this technique, the better it works. If you focus on mindful breathing in the present moment, you won't focus on fretting about the future, you'll be psyching yourself up to perform.

One Final Thought

Opening night of a stage play is thrilling for the actors. The rehearsal hall has given way to a theater with sets, costumes, and bright lights, and the audience reacts in unexpected, exciting ways. There is applause, and the anticipation of reviews. But opening night's adrenaline soon dissipates, and second performances with tired actors can be a letdown. There is a lesson to be learned in this pitfall, as the following anecdote testifies.

A veteran stage director gathered his cast before every second performance for a pep talk. "Long ago when I was a young dancer in vaudeville," he would say, "I was in a show that included a flock of dancing flamingos. Their 'dressing room' was a pen in the wings, where they heard everything that happened onstage. When their entrance music played, they began to squawk, flap their wings, and leap in the air with excitement. Those flamingos couldn't wait to get onstage and perform." Then he paused dramatically, looked at each actor in the cast and said, "Birds! Damn it—birds can get up for a performance. So go out there tonight and break a leg!"

The moral of this story? If birds can psych themselves up to perform, so can you. If flamingos can learn to dance, so too can you train yourself to stand still, gesture artfully, and control the pace of your delivery. With inspiration tempered by discipline, your presentations will be masterly, and language—perhaps humanity's greatest achievement—will take wing and soar.

Summary

Practice really does work, and produces tangible results in a surprisingly short time. Ask any professional athlete or musician. If you've managed to read this far without actually trying any of the exercises suggested, put down the book and give it a whirl.

Practice is the only way to improve any skill. It is the ultimate skill, allowing you to turn what you know into the solid performance skill of know-how. Conquer any resistance you may feel about practicing and learn to do it alone, aloud, and a lot. Remember, you are not prepping yourself to be perfect; you are practicing to get better. Be patient and methodical. It doesn't have to take hours every day. Short sessions may be more productive.

Create notes to serve as a visual aid that will allow you to refine the skill of structured improvisation. As you begin, run up the body's checklist from feet to head. Warm up your articulators so those muscles are ready to work. Give special energy and attention to rehearsing beginnings and endings. Once you decide what you wish to say to begin, train yourself to jump-start your instinct to gesture.

Practice with your visual aids, and if you intend to read from a document, read it numerous times, deliberately and with meaning. If you have a particular skill you are attempting to improve, take ten minutes a day to focus exclusively on that skill.

In addition to formal practice sessions, use speaking opportunities in everyday life—informal practice—to improve your ability to communicate fluently and articulately. Carefully observe other speakers; adopt and adapt the skills you see used by gifted communicators. Understand and avoid those problems that make mediocre presenters less effective. Psych yourself up to speak. Discover the excitement and satisfaction in doing it well.

Talk to Yourself

"Just five minutes of practice builds confidence."

"I need to practice out loud using these notes to make sure they work."

"I'm stuck in traffic! I'll practice the beginning of my speech several times."

"In this conversation I will eliminate 'um' and think in silence."

"During lunch with colleagues I'll be more aware of my eye contact."

"During this phone call I will walk down the steps to sound confident."

"Talking too fast is just a habit that I can break during this meeting."

"I practiced my conclusion, so I can jump to it if I run out of time."

Appendices

Appendix One

Speaker's Checklist

Coordinating your body, your brain, and your voice for effective speaking

Controlling Your Body

- Before you stand up to speak, get conscious control of your breath by inhaling deeply and exhaling slowly.
- Continue to breathe deeply and slowly as you walk to the front of the room.
- Relax your facial expression; release any tension from your mouth or eyebrows.
- Adopt a dynamic stance: center your weight evenly on both feet.
- Don't slouch or lean on lecterns or tables.
- Look up from your notes and make eye contact with your listeners before you start talking.
- Systematically look at those seated at the four corners of the audience perimeter.
- Place your hands in a ready position, touching loosely at waist height with elbows bent at 90 degrees.
- Get the arms ready to gesture before you speak, then instruct your body to release the gestures as you talk.
- Inhale consciously one last time before uttering your first sentence. This breath will support and project your voice. Breathe in, speak out.
- Remember the three Rs of natural gesturing: *ready* to gesture, *release* gestures, and *relax* your arms at your sides occasionally.
- Channel the adrenaline created by exhilaration and/or anxiety into big, smooth gestures.
- Gestures that are larger in size and longer in duration will make you feel and appear more natural.
- Get some "air in the armpits" and your gestures will look and feel more natural.
- Gesture from the shoulder, not just from the elbow.
- Plan and practice an initial trigger gesture to help jump-start your natural instinct to gesture.
- Trigger gestures: *give* (facts or questions), *chop* (emphasis), or *show* (on the one hand...on the other hand).

- Smoothly fill your natural zone of gesture: a rectangular space approximately four feet wide by two feet high.
- Gesture with open hands and open palms; don't curl your fingers inward.
- When asking questions, use the palms up, questioning gesture.
- Once you jump-start your initial gestures, stop thinking about them and let your instinct take over.

Controlling Your Brain

- Don't tell yourself to "Relax!" Instead, raise and release your energy level as you begin speaking.
- To get your brain focused, talk to people, not paper. Don't look at your notes during the first few sentences.
- Imagine you are speaking with individuals, not talking to an impersonal, monolithic audience.
- Don't be surprised by your listeners' stoic, deadpan facial expressions. (It has nothing to do with you!)
- Recognize the time warp created by adrenaline; plan to speak slowly at the start to compensate for your altered perception of time.
- Pauses are good; silence is golden. Short pauses give you time to think ahead and listeners time to absorb.
- Lay out the structure of your presentation for your audience. Saying it aloud will help you remember it too.
- Reveal your enthusiasm and interest in your subject, and be appropriately friendly.
- Realize that your audience can't tell how nervous you are inside; take comfort in that realization.
- Be patient and don't hit the panic button when you need to mentally search for your next word or idea.
- Use headlines to announce new topics: "Now let's focus on..."
- When using notes, less is more! Use bullet points. Resist reading from your notes.
- Don't be afraid to look at your notes between topics. Listeners only object when you talk to your notes.
- Notes are a visual aid for you, so write big, and keep them simple.
- Try using horizontal notes.
- Put notes where they are easy to see.

Controlling Your Voice

- Breathe deeply and vigorously! The power of your speaking voice is proportional to your breath support.

- To control the pace, speak in phrases, not whole sentences. Use the rhythm of the *Pledge of Allegiance.*

- Vary the pace: speak in phrases on important points, and speak more briskly for introductory material.

- Control any unconscious thinking noises—*um* and *uh*—by consciously substituting silence instead.

- Emphasis creates meaning; speak dynamically to stress the key word or phrases in every sentence.

- Recognize that words deserving emphasis are often at ends of sentences.

- Emphasize the endings of your sentences to keep your voice from trailing off.

- Beware the pitfall of ending sentences with a repetitive rising inflection, which sounds like you are asking a question or making a list.

- Lower the pitch of your voice (not the volume) when ending sentences to sound confident and conclusive.

- Avoid excessive use of the conjunction "and" to connect your sentences and questions.

- Escape monotone delivery by putting emphatic stress on key words to stimulate natural inflection.

- Slow down and speak in more deliberate phrases when discussing complicated issues.

Practicing Aloud

- Practice on your feet to coordinate your body, brain, and voice.

- Practice aloud to build the muscle memory of your articulators: lips, tongue, jaw.

- Rough draft aloud: talk first, write second.

- Practice aloud behind the wheel when you are driving in your car.

- Don't practice talking to a mirror! Mirrors merely make you more self-conscious.

- Practice aloud, alone, a lot!

- If you have limited time, always practice the first paragraph aloud, several times, so you can start strong.

- If you have limited time, always practice the last paragraph aloud, several times, so you can end strong.

Appendix Two

Video Self-Review Checklist
Critiquing yourself on video

Feet & Stance

- Is your stance dynamic? Are your feet a comfortable distance apart?
- Is your body weight centered so it is evenly balanced over both feet?
- Watch to see if you stand still at the beginning.
- Are your ankles crossed? Uncross them!
- Notice whether your feet are shuffling or shifting. Move only with a purpose, not randomly; walk to a new location when changing topics.
- Shifting only a couple of feet looks like nervous fidgeting. Move at least six feet when you decide to walk to a new location.
- Look at your feet. Are they moving more than your arms? Feet tend to shuffle or pace too much when the arms gesture too little. Think: Let your arms do the walking.

Knees & Hips

- Knees should be flexible, not locked, as they are when you are standing in a moving bus or subway.
- Your hips should be centered over your feet. Avoid resting your weight on one hip, leaning casually to one side.

Breath Support

- Observe your breathing. Breathe consciously before you stand up; this helps to control the adrenaline rush and calm your nerves.
- Can you see your lungs expanding and contracting? Breathe deeply from your abdominal area to project your voice and flood your brain with oxygen.

Gestures

- Are your hands in a ready position? Hands should be touching at your navel, elbows bent 90 degrees.

- Avoid the fig leaf position, reverse fig leaf, hands in your pockets, or holding your pen. (You may click and fondle the pen, and be the only one who doesn't realize it).

- Gestures should be larger in size and longer in duration in order to look and feel natural.

- Natural gestures are smoother rather than jerkier, and slower rather than faster. Think smooth and slow.

- When do you begin to gesture? Consciously gesture sooner rather than later. Jump-start gestures immediately.

- Do you use the "on the one hand... on the other hand" gesture to trigger your instinct to gesture?

- You should fill the zone of gesture: a 2'x 4' rectangle, two feet from your waist to your chin, and four feet out to the sides.

- Watch for show gestures. Could your hands be more expressive?

- Look for the karate chop or double karate chop with your hands sideways for the most emphatic delivery.

- If there is a lectern, are you touching it? Don't lean on the lectern with locked elbows, shoving your shoulders up toward your ears. Don't slouch on the lectern, placing your forearms on the furniture. Stand up straight at the lectern.

- Observe whether you drop your arms to your sides—the release position—as you finish a thought. Be your own exclamation mark!

Posture

- Look at your body's alignment. Good posture is not shoulders back and chest out! That increases tension.

- Good posture is a direction—upward—not a position that is held like a statue.

- Your head belongs over your torso, not out front in a "chicken neck" position (don't lift your chin).

- Imagine your head is being pulled upward by a bungee cord attached to the top of your skull.

Face

- Is your face alive? Adopt your natural face of "introduction," the one you use when you shake hands introducing yourself.
- Beware the deadpan "cadaver face." Try parting your lips slightly.
- Breathe through your mouth and nose.
- Notice whether your face and gestures are working together. Natural gestures tend to bring natural animation to your facial expressions.
- Don't freeze up! Keep gesturing.

Eyes

- Are you looking at your listeners? Did you focus on the audience before you began speaking?
- You should look at the four corners of the perimeter of your audience to define the target area.
- Understand your "thinking mannerism": When considering what to say next, do you look up, down, or sideways? Don't look away from people for too long.
- Focus your eyes to focus your brain.

Thinking

- Don't read to them! Talk to them. Which are you doing?
- Are there pauses in your delivery? Silence is golden. Silence is your friend.
- Adrenaline's time warp makes pauses seem inordinately long.
- Have you given both yourself and your listeners time to think?
- Time your pauses. How many seconds pass during each one? One second? Two?
- Where are you looking? Don't start by looking at and reading from your notes. Focus on the people you are addressing.
- You should use your notes like a parachute; go to them if you are about to crash and burn.
- Are your notes easy to read? Construct your notes as a visual aid for yourself: write big and keep it simple.
- Check to see whether you have defaulted to a furrowed brow.
- Actively choose your attitude. Attitude is a tactical choice.

Speaking

- You should hear yourself speak in phrases, not whole sentences. As you begin, use the pace of the *Pledge of Allegiance*.

- Listen to your pace. Start slowly by speaking in phrases, then speed up as you get comfortable.

- A slow pace signals the importance of what you are saying. Emphatic points should be slower.

- Have you varied your pace? Separate... every... word occasionally to achieve a super-slow pace for extra emphasis.

- Speaking too softly? Use more breath support.

- Is your voice trailing off? Emphasize the final word or phrase in questions.

- Beware of the questioning uptick of inflection at the ends of sentences. It makes you sound uncertain.

- Do you drop the pitch of your voice to end sentences conclusively?

- Think of how newscasters sign off at the end of a broadcast. Listen to hear whether you walk down the steps.

The Law of Opposites

- Have you applied the Law of Opposites? For a sentence or even just a phrase, have you done the opposite of what your instinct most often leads you to do?

- Listen carefully to hear whether you go slower than your usual pace for emphasis, or speak softer than your usual volume for emphasis.

- Make sure that you are still on occasion, not just animated.

- Listen for contrast. Do you ever use longer silences to let the audience think?

- Notice whether the "s" words could apply to your performance: slower, softer, stiller, and silence.

Bibliography

Alibali, Martha W., Miriam Bassok, Karen Olseth Solomon, Sharon E. Syc, and Susan Goldin-Meadow. "Illuminating Mental Representations through Speech and Gesture." *Psychological Science* 10, no. 4 (July 1999): 327–33.

Amberry, Tom, and Philip Reed. *Free Throw: 7 Steps to Success at the Free Throw Line.* New York: HarperCollins, 1996.

Burns, Ken. *The Civil War,* film. Washington, D.C.: Public Broadcasting Service, 1990.

Gawande, Atul. *Complications: A Surgeon's Notes on an Imperfect Science.* New York: Picador, 2002.

Goldin-Meadow, Susan. *Hearing Gesture: How Our Hands Help Us Think.* Cambridge, MA: Belknap Press, 2003.

Holzer, Harold. *Lincoln at Cooper Union: The Speech That Made Abraham Lincoln President.* New York: Simon & Schuster, 2004.

Iverson, Jana M. "Gesture When There Is No Visual Model." In *The Nature and Functions of Gesture in Children's Communication: New Directions for Child Development, No. 79,* edited by Jana M. Iverson and Susan Goldin-Meadow, 89–100. San Francisco: Jossey-Bass, Spring 1998.

Jackson, Susan A., and Mihaly Csikszentmihalyi. *Flow in Sports: The Keys to Optimal Experiences and Performances.* Champaign, IL: Human Kinetics, 1999.

Kendon, Adam. "An Agenda for Gesture Studies." *Semiotic Review of Books 7,* no. 3 (1996): 8–12. http://projects.chass.utoronto.ca /semiotics/srb/gesture.html.

Kendon, Adam, ed. "Gesture and Understanding in Social Interaction." Special issue, *Research on Language and Social Interaction* 27, no. 3 (1994).

McNeill, David. *Hand and Mind: What Gestures Reveal about Thought.* Chicago: University of Chicago Press, 1992.

"Mirror Neurons." *NOVA scienceNOW.* PBS Video, 13:50. Premiered January 1, 2005. http://video.pbs.org/video/1615173073.

Ornstein, Robert E. *On the Experience of Time.* Boulder, CO: Westview Press, 1997.

Tufte, Edward R. *The Cognitive Style of PowerPoint: Pitching Out Corrupts Within.* 2nd ed. Cheshire, CT: Graphics Press, 2006.

Wills, Garry. *Lincoln at Gettysburg: The Words That Remade America.* New York: Touchstone, 1992.

Wilson, Frank R. *The Hand: How Its Use Shapes the Brain, Language, and Human Culture.* New York: Pantheon Books, 1998.

Index

A

adrenaline
  blushing and eye contact, 56–57
  body and, 7, 10–12
  brain and, 62
  as energy source, 59
  heart rate and, 64–65
  holding a pen and, 38
  random movement and, 19
  standing still and, 16
  time warp and, 62–64
alignment, posture and alignment,
  49–53, 176
alternative positions, hands, 36
Amberry, Tom, 12–13
anxiety and gestures, 31–32
articulation and voice, 105–108
attention and structured presentations,
  85–88
attitude as tactical choice, 88–90'
audible punctuation, 134–136

B

baton gestures, 39
beginnings
  deliberate sentence beginnings, 117
  practicing, 148–149
  practicing beginnings with gestures,
  130–132
behavior, conscious control of, 12,
  59–60
being yourself, 6, 8
blushing and eye contact, 56–57
body
  adrenaline and, 7, 10–12
  body control checklist, 171–172
  breathing in and speaking out,
  24–25
  centering your hips, 17–18, 175
  conscious breathing mechanics,
  22–24, 175
  knee flexibility, 16–17, 175
  lower body control, 14–20
  oxygenation of brain, 25
  paradox of naturalness and, 7, 8
  performance rituals and, 12–14
  planting your feet, 15–16, 175
  posture and alignment, 49–53
  purposeful movement, 19–21
  ritual movement and conscious
  breathing, 21–22
  standing still, 16, 156
  and your face, 53–58
  See also gestures; hands
brain
  adrenaline and, 62
  brain control checklist, 172
  echo memory, 67–68
  gestures and language, 26–28
  mirror neurons and, 90–91
  oxygenation of, 25
  paradox of naturalness and, 7–8
  prefrontal cortex and physical rituals, 13
  speaking in phrases and, 111, 115
  zone of concentration and, 65–67
  See also presentations
breathing
  breathe in and speak out, 24–25
  conscious breathing and ritual
  movement, 21–22
  conscious breathing mechanics,
  22–24
  larynx and vocal cords, 105
  lungs and diaphragm, 22–23,
  101–103
  oxygenation of brain and, 25
  projecting your voice, 103–104

C

centering your hips, 17–18
chop gestures, 41–46, 47–49
chunking information, 84
Complications (Gawande), 56–57
comprehension and gestures, 27–28
confidence
    instilling in listeners, 1–2
    public speaking and, 10
conscious breathing
    breathing in and speaking out, 24–25
    mechanics, 22–24
    oxygenation of brain and, 25
    ritual movement and, 21–22
conscious gestures, 29–30
control
    body control checklist, 171–172
    brain control checklist, 172
    breath control, 24
    voice control checklist, 173
Croft, Peter, 65

D

deep breathing, 22–23
deliberate sentence beginnings, 117
distracting gestures, 39

E

echo memory, 67–68
elocution, 106–108
eloquent speech and silence, 109
emotions and breathing, 21
emphasis
    emphasis and meaning, 120–127
    gestures and emphasis, 127–133
energy and pacing of speech, 109–110
expressions and your face, 53
eyes
    blushing and eye contact, 56–57
    eye contact, 20, 55–58
    focused gaze, 157
    and looking at notes, 58
    video self-review checklist, 177

F

face
    eye contact, 55–58
    forehead and brow, 54–55
    mouth, 53–54
    video self-review checklist, 177
fatigue, vocal fatigue, 104
Federer, Roger, 65
feet, planting your feet, 15–16, 175
    See also presentations
fig leaf position, hands, 34
fight-or-flight syndrome, 11, 57, 62–63
finger wagging, 39
flexibility, knee flexibility, 16–17
forehead and brow, 54–55
forgetting, planning to forget, 80–83
Free Throw (Amberry), 13
furrowed brow, 54–55

G

gestures
    distracting gestures, 39
    gestures and emphasis, 127–133
    gesturing immediately, 148
    give, chop, and show, 41–46
    horizontal notes and, 73–79
    impulse to gesture, 32–33
    jump-starting, 29, 59–60
    natural gestures, 26–28
    practicing, 28, 29–30, 49
    the ready position, 37
    "on the shelf" gestures, 46–48,
    75–79
    speaking and, 25–26
    three Rs of natural gestures, 40–41
    video self-review checklist, 176
    zone of gesture, 30–32
give, chop, and show gestures, 41–46,
    47–49
Goldin-Meadow, Susan, 28, 30–31

H

Hand and Mind (McNeill), 28
The Hand (Wilson), 28

hands
    alternative positions, 36
    and holding a pen, 38
    impulse to gesture and, 33
    mechanics of readiness, 36–37
    and the ready position, 33–38
    and the secret handshake, 37–38
    See also gestures
"having butterflies in your stomach",
    11
head
    neck and head, 50
    spine alignment and, 50–52
Hearing Gesture (Goldin-Meadow), 28,
    30–31
heart rate and adrenaline, 64–65
high heels and centering your hips, 18
hips, centering your hips, 17–18
holding a pen, 38
horizontal notes, 73–79

I

improvisation, structured improvisa-
    tion, 69–70
impulse to gesture, 32–33
information, chunking information, 84
intonation, 133–134
invisible ready position, 34–36
Iverson, Jana, 26–27, 127

J

Jamail, Joe, 1

K

Kendon, Adam, 27
Kennedy, John F., 113, 125
King, Martin Luther, Jr., 125
knee flexibility, 16–17

L

language and gestures, 26–28
larynx and vocal cords, 105
law of opposites and speaking style,
    162–163, 178
lips

articulation and, 105–106
    "neutral alert" face, 53–54
listeners
    gestures and, 26
    horizontal notes and, 78–79
    instilling confidence in, 1–2
    show gestures and, 45
    silence and, 66–67
    stoic faces of, 56
    structured presentations and, 85–88
looking at notes, 58
lower body control, 14–20
lungs and diaphragm, 22–23, 101–103

M

mannerisms
    adrenaline and, 12
    paradox of naturalness and, 7
McLuhan, Marshall, 88
meaning, emphasis and meaning,
    120–127
mechanics of readiness, 36–37
memory
    echo memory, 67–68
    reciting from memory, 151–152
minding the gap, 119–120, 158
mirror neurons, 90–91
monotone and absence of gestures,
    128–129
mouth, 53–54
movement, purposeful movement,
    19–21
muscles
    conscious control of, 18, 19
    muscle memory and gestures, 29–30
    respiration and, 101–103
    zone of concentration and, 65

N

natural gestures, 26–28
naturalness, paradox of, 6–8
neck and head, 50
nervous system, respiratory system
    control, 22

"neutral alert" face, 53–54
notes
   handy access to, 72–73
   horizontal notes, 73–79
   large font and, 72
   legibility, 73–74
   looking at notes, 58
   practicing with, 80, 96
   practicing with notes and visual aids, 152–154
   reading from notes, 68–69, 80
   simplicity of, 72–73

O

On the Experience of Time (Ornstein), 63
"on the shelf" gestures, 46–48
oxygenation of brain, 25

P

pacing
   energy and pacing of speech, 109–110
   eye contact and, 58
   gestures and conducting yourself, 129
   phrasing mechanics, 112–114
   purposeful movement and, 16
   setting the pace, 115–116
   speaking pace, 8
   speaking too quickly and, 156–157
   variations in speaking pace, 114–115
paradox of naturalness, 6–8
pen, holding a pen, 38
performance pressure and adrenaline, 10–12
performance rituals and the body, 12–14
phrasing
   phrasing mechanics, 112–114
   speaking in phrases, 110–112, 147
pitch
   audible punctuation and, 134–136
   intonation and, 133–134
   volume, pitch, and duration, 124–126
planning to forget, 80–83
planting your feet, 15–16
pointing at audience, 39
posture and alignment, 49–53, 176
PowerPoint, 91–95
practicing
   alone, aloud, and a lot, 140–141, 173–174
   beginnings, 148–149
   endings, 149–150
   focused gaze, 157
   gestures, 28, 29–30, 41–46, 49, 148, 156
   informal practice sessions, 160–161
   inhibitory rationalizations, 143–144
   mental preparation and, 163–165
   need for, 140, 141–142, 165–166
   with notes, 80, 96, 152–154
   patience and, 144
   physical rituals and body checklist, 59–60, 146
   practicing in the actual room, 145
   reading aloud and, 150–151
   recitation and, 151–152
   resistance and avoidance, 142–144
   speaking in phrases, 147
   speaking too quickly, 156–157
   speaking too softly, 155–156
   standing still, 156
   talk first and write second, 148
   thinking noise elimination, 8, 117–120, 158–159
   transitions, 150
   and using a mirror, 142–143
   verbal skills and, 3–4, 97, 136–138, 167
   videotaping and, 154, 175–178
   visualizing your performance, 132–133
   warming up your voice, 147

presentations
attitude and, 88–90
avoid thinking backward, 83–84
chunking information, 84
planning to forget, 80–83
PowerPoint and, 91–95
purposeful movement and, 19
reading and talking simultaneously, 71
reading from notes, 68–69, 80
recitation, 69
scripting as preliminary step, 83
structured improvisation, 69–70
structured presentations (primacy and recency), 85–88, 96
video self-review checklist, 177
visualizing your performance, 132–133
See also notes; practicing; voice
primacy and structured presentations, 85–88, 96
projecting your voice, 103–104
prosody and natural conversation, 133–136
public speaking skills
need for, 1–2, 5–6
projecting your voice, 103–104
training, 2–3
vocal fatigue, 104
See also practicing; voice
punctuation, audible punctuation, 134–136
purposeful movement, 19–21

Q
questioning gesture, give gestures, 42–43

R
random movement and adrenaline, 19
readiness mechanics, 36–37
reading
PowerPoint and, 95
practicing reading aloud, 150–151
reading and talking simultaneously, 71
reading from notes, 68–69, 80
when to read aloud, 126–127
the ready position, hands, 33–38
ready, three Rs of natural gestures, 40–41
recency and structured presentations, 85–88, 96
recitation, 69, 83–84, 151–152
relax, three Rs of natural gestures, 40–41
release, three Rs of natural gestures, 40–41
respiratory system
muscles, 101–103
nervous system control of, 22
rhythm
phrasing mechanics, 112–114
prosody and natural conversation, 133–136
rituals, performance rituals and the body, 12–14, 59
rocking and centering your hips, 17
Rodenburg, Patsy, 24

S
scripting as preliminary step, 83
the secret handshake, 37–38
Shakespeare on gestures, 28
show gestures, 41–46, 47–49
silence
conscious behavior control and, 12
echo memory and, 68
eloquent speech and, 109
presentations and, 96
speaking too quickly and, 156–157
zone of concentration and, 66–67
sitting, speaking while sitting, 52
smooth gestures, 129–130
speaking
gestures and, 26–28
mental preparation and, 163–165

speaking in phrases, 110–112, 147
speaking too quickly, 62, 65–66
video self-review checklist, 178
while sitting, 52
See also practicing; presentations;
  voice
spine alignment, 50–52
stance, planting your feet, 15–16, 175
standing still, 16, 19, 156
structured improvisation, 69–70, 96
structured presentations (primacy and
  recency), 85–88
style
  gestures and, 28
  law of opposites and, 162–163, 178
  purposeful movement and, 20
"subway knees", 16

T
talking to yourself, 97
technique and paradox of naturalness,
  8
tension
  furrowed brow, 54–55
  mouth and lips, 53–54
thinking and brain oxygenation, 25
thinking noises
  elimination of, 8, 117–120, 158–
  159
  zone of concentration and, 65–66
thinking on your feet. *See* presentations
thought processes. *See* brain
three Rs of natural gestures, 40–41
thumb puppet gestures, 39
the time warp
  adrenaline and, 62–64
  speaking in phrases and, 111
  zone of concentration and, 65–67
"tucking the tail bone", 18

U
unnatural behaviors, 6

V
videotaping and practicing, 154,
175–178
visualization, show gestures, 44–46
visualizing your performance, 132–133
vocal fatigue, 104
voice
  articulation and, 105–108
  deliberate sentence beginnings, 117
  emphasis and meaning, 120–127
  energy and pacing of speech,
  109–110
  gestures and emphasis, 127–133
  larynx and vocal cords, 105
  listening to yourself and, 100–101
  lungs and diaphragm, 101–103
  paradox of naturalness and, 8
  phrasing mechanics, 112–114
  practicing verbal skills, 136–138
  projecting your voice, 103–104
  prosody and natural conversation,
  133–136
  setting the pace, 115–116
  speaking in phrases, 110–112
  thinking noise elimination, 117–120
  variations in speaking pace, 114–
  115
  vocal fatigue, 104
  voice control checklist, 173
  volume, pitch, and duration,
  124–126
  warming up, 106–108, 147
volume of voice, 8, 124–126

W
warming up your voice, 106–108, 147

Z
zone of concentration and the brain,
  65–67
zone of gesture, 30–32

About the Authors

BRIAN K. JOHNSON has worked as a communication consultant to the legal profession since 1979, teaching persuasion to trial lawyers and public speaking to transactional attorneys. Every year he works one-on-one with hundreds of attorneys to help them analyze and improve their skills. His international consulting practice takes him to elite law firms and training programs throughout the U.S. and Canada, as well as overseas to the United Kingdom and Europe. He has taught Solicitor Advocates in Belfast, Northern Ireland and Dublin, Ireland, and has twice trained federal prosecutors for the Republic of Estonia.

For the past decade Johnson has trained all new Assistant United States Attorneys at the Department of Justice National Advocacy Center. He has been a communication specialist for the National Institute for Trial Advocacy since 1981. In 2000, NITA recognized his unique contribution to the teaching of advocacy skills by presenting him with the Honorable Prentice Marshall Faculty Award. He was the first non-lawyer in NITA history to receive this honor. For 25 years his courtroom communication skills lecture/demonstration with Marsha Hunter has kicked off the NITA National Trial Skills Session in Boulder, Colorado.

MARSHA HUNTER teaches persuasion for trial lawyers and public speaking for corporate attorneys. She works exclusively with lawyers. Her specialty is human factors—the science of human performance in high-stakes environments. Hunter's expertise in cognition and communication focuses on how people think, speak, feel, and act in dynamic situations. Her teaching is both technical and practical, drawing on techniques from sports psychology, linguistics, and cognitive science.

Three times each year, Hunter is the program director for *The Articulate Advocate®: Becoming More Fluent on Your Feet,* a two-day intensive courtroom communication skills program, at NITA's National Education Center in Boulder, Colorado. Ms. Hunter is the communication specialist for NITA's collaborative programs with the U.S. Department of Justice's Office of Violence Against Women, and teaches at regional trial skills programs annually for NITA. She trains at the Department of Justice's National Advocacy Center in Columbia, South Carolina. She has served on preparation teams for lawyers appearing in multiple cases before the Ninth Circuit and the U.S. Supreme Court, and taught advocacy programs for the Law Society of Upper Canada, the Law Society of Northern Ireland, and the Law Society of Tasmania. Her in-house clients include firms that occupy the top 10, 50, and 100 in annual lists, and half of the Wall Street Journal's "fearsome foursome" of litigation.

Hunter has published articles in many legal publications, including the American Bar Association Section of Litigation's *The Woman Advocate* and the *Texas Bar Journal*.

Johnson and Hunter are co-authors of *The Articulate Advocate: New Techniques of Persuasion for Trial Lawyers* (Crown King Books, 2009), a 2010 Silver Medal winner in the Benjamin Franklin Awards from the Independent Book Publishers Association, and *The Articulate Attorney: Public Speaking for Lawyers* (Crown King Books, 2010, 2013).